SPICECRAFTS

SPICECRAFTS

INSPIRATIONS FOR PRACTICAL GIFTS, CRAFTS AND DISPLAYS

TESSA EVELEGH

PHOTOGRAPHS BY MICHELLE GARRETT

LORENZ BOOKS
NEW YORK • LONDON • SYDNEY • BATH

This edition published in the UK in 1997 by Lorenz Books
This edition published in the USA by Lorenz Books
27 West 20th Steet, New York, New York 10011; (800) 354-9657

LORENZ BOOKS are available for bulk purchase for sales promotion and for premium use.
For details write or call the manager of special sales:
Lorenz Books, 27 West 20th Street, New York New York 10011; (800) 354-9657.

ISBN 1 85967 494 1

Publisher: Joanna Lorenz
Project Editor: Joanne Rippin
Designer: Nigel Partridge

Printed and bound in Singapore
1 3 5 7 9 10 8 6 4 2

CONTENTS

INTRODUCTION

…there were gardens bright with sinuous rills, Where blossomed many an incense-bearing tree…
SAMUEL TAYLOR COLERIDGE (1772–1834), KUBLA KHAN

Pungent and aromatic, spices have been so highly valued that they have changed the course of history itself. Wars have been fought for them, continents discovered and subterfuges employed to keep their whereabouts secret, such has been the power of what are essentially the dried up parts of plants. But, packed into the bark, roots, tiny seeds, flowers, and even stamens of these prized plants is an explosion of flavour that has been used to lend piquancy to food since ancient times. Prized over the centuries for scenting and healing as well as flavouring, spices have come to represent the epitome of anything exciting.

Yet nowadays, we use spices for very little other than flavouring. Endless books are written about the culinary uses of these aromatic treasures; few delve into other uses for them. The general impression of spices from a visual standpoint is that they are very often rather small, brown and dried up. But even small, brown and dried up can look stunning when used cleverly; and, in fact, the variety of the colours and shapes of spices provides plenty of scope. Fleshy red chilli peppers and elegant rolled cinnamon sticks offer great possibilities, as do some of the less obvious

The elegant, rich coloured quills of cinnamon are one of the most decorative spices.

materials, such as cool green cardamom pods, vibrant red peppertree berries, lacy mace and textural nutmegs. Integral to all spices is a glorious aroma, ensuring that most things you make with them will scent the room with their exotic perfume. Apart from the sheer pleasure of these natural room fragrances, according to the theories of aromatherapy, spices can also be.mood enhancing, many of them having a relaxing effect, while others are stimulating or uplifting.

There are no particular skills needed for working with spices, but you may well find you can apply your own particular interests to spicecrafts. If you love to sew, try some of the aromatic cushions, sachets or padded

coathangers; if dried flowers are more your style, you will enjoy making the wreaths, topiaries and garlands. Cooks can bottle up spicy fruits, oils, vinegars, pickles and peppers, following the recipes specially created for the book, and party-givers may like to set some spicy dinner tables or create aromatic Christmas decorations.

It is not difficult to find the raw materials for spicecrafts, but, depending on what you choose to make, you may need to find a supplier of spices in bulk. Asian supermarkets are a particularly good source as they often sell a wide range of spices in large packets for very reasonable prices. Alternatively, you could go direct to the wholesalers. Dried-flower specialists are another useful supplier for spicecrafts, as they supply cinnamon sticks, dried chillies and, sometimes, boxes of cloves and star anise. They also sell foam bases for topiary and willow wreath-bases.

Whatever your own skills, this book will inspire you to look at spices in a new and exciting way, and to add colour, passion, flavour and excitement to your home.

RIGHT: Spices can be used to create endless fragrant treats, from pomanders to cushions.

CHAPTER ONE

THE HISTORY OF SPICES

THERE CAME NO MORE SUCH ABUNDANCE

OF SPICES AS THESE WHICH THE QUEEN OF SHEBA

GAVE TO KING SOLOMON.

1 KINGS 10:10

ABOVE AND LEFT: Piles of spices which you might find in Indian markets, ranging from bright yellows and reds to softest greens and earthy browns, make a vibrant sight.

THE ANCIENTS

The centuries-old quest for spices testifies to their tremendous worth in ancient times. They were seen to hold the very key to a healthy and enjoyable life, providing medicines, perfumes and flavourings for food. Even in death, they had their value – those who could afford them used them for embalming. Spices were so highly prized that traders down the ages were prepared to cross vast and often hostile oceans and continents to secure them, fight wars and even weave fantastical fables around them to safeguard the secret of their whereabouts.

Spices are first mentioned in the Bible in about 1900 BC being carried on camels by the traders who had bought Joseph from his brothers. These traders were Ishmaelites,

BELOW: The Queen of Sheba showered gifts of spices on the powerful King Solomon.

carrying their wares on the final leg of the spice trail to their destination in Egypt.

The long trail began in China where the precious spices were brought from the rain forests of South-east Asia. They were carried by nomads south of the Gobi Desert, across northern India to the Middle East, where Arabian caravans would trade them for gold, silver and gems. The Arabs controlled the spice trade for centuries, supplying all the ancient civilizations of the Mediterranean region, and they were prepared to employ subterfuge to retain their command over these valuable commodities. In order to keep secret the true Oriental origin of cassia – a spice like cinnamon widely used in the ancient world – they constructed a fanciful description of its harvest, which was faithfully recorded by the Greek historian, Herodotus. The rolls of bark, they reported, were brought to Arabia by large birds to build their nests. Hunters tempted the birds with large pieces of meat, which they seized and carried up to their nests. When the nests broke, the hunters were able to collect the cassia for market.

As well as indigenous spices such as poppy seed and coriander, Roman and Greek

ABOVE: Spices were carried by a relay of caravans across northern India where they were met by Arabian traders who distributed them throughout the Middle East and the Roman Empire.

cuisines were rich in spices brought from the East to flavour foods and make medicines and perfumes. Saffron from Asia Minor, still today the most expensive spice in the world, was sometimes used to strew in the paths of visiting kings and princes. Emperor Nero was reported to have burned more incense and cassia on his wife's funeral pyre than Arabia was able to produce in a year. Later, early in the fifth century, 300 pounds of peppercorns were paid to Alaric, King of the Visigoths, as a ransom for Rome.

The Romans introduced spices all over their vast empire, though the supplies were cut off when they left and it wasn't until the first Crusaders returned from the Middle East early in the twelfth century that these aromatics could be enjoyed again in northern Europe and the British Isles. By this time, Venice had control of the Orient's spice trade with Europe and of the gold travelling east. She retained this powerful position until the fall of Constantinople (Istanbul) to the Ottoman Empire in 1453, which cut Venice off from the ancient overland trade routes.

THE SPICE TRADE IN THE COLONIAL AGE

Spicy aromas and flavourings from the Far East had become firmly established in Europe by the time the Ottoman Empire obstructed the spice trade, and the quest for access to spices demanded a renewed effort. Within 40 years, the need for sea-borne trade had led to the development of more sophisticated ships, which made way for the great voyages of discovery of the fifteenth century. In 1492, Christopher Columbus headed west, thinking he could sail around the world to reach India. Instead, he landed in the Bahamas, discovering in the "West Indies" chillies, allspice berries and vanilla pods.

In 1497, Vasco da Gama set out from Portugal and headed east, becoming the first navigator to round the Cape of Good Hope and reach India by sea. The Portuguese were now able to exploit the cinnamon of Ceylon (Sri Lanka). Further east, in Indonesia, they occupied the Moluccas (Spice Islands), set up a trading post in Malacca on the Malay Peninsula and shipped pepper, cloves, nutmeg and mace back to Lisbon.

Far more devastating for the Moluccans

RIGHT: Ferdinand and Isabella of Spain receive Christopher Columbus on his return in 1493.

ABOVE: The Dutch East India Company fleet received a tumultuous welcome at its homecoming.

was the arrival of the Dutch in 1612, who took radical steps to keep spice prices high in Europe. They were so successful with the cloves that they produced a glut and ended up with a ten-year supply in warehouses in Amsterdam, which had to be burned to protect their investment. In 1625 they destroyed all the clove trees, except for those on the island of Amboyna, reducing the population of the other islands to poverty because they were no longer able to trade cloves for rice.

The nutmeg trees were to suffer a similar fate and a few years later, in 1636, the Dutch tried to secure a monopoly of cinnamon in Ceylon by destroying not only all the wild trees on the island but those on the Indian Malabar coast too. For nearly two centuries, they used ruthless tactics to keep a tight control on the trade of spices. Nevertheless, the Company went bankrupt in 1799, about twenty years after clove and nutmeg seedlings had been smuggled out of the Spice Islands by a French botanist and planted in Mauritius and other French colonies. By the beginning of the nineteenth century no European power had a monopoly on any spice and prices began to fall at last.

BENEFICIAL SPICES

Spices, as well as herbs, were used in traditional folk medicines, and it is true that the advance of modern science has isolated the beneficial properties of many "old wives'" remedies. Now that some people are becoming disenchanted with "conventional" medicine, they are turning back to the older, holistic, herbal methods, which treat the whole person rather than a specific set of symptoms. Most herbal therapies seek to create a balance in the whole body, rather than looking for symptoms indicating a particular illness and treating them with particular remedies. This results in often vague-sounding medicinal uses for spices, some of which are listed in the Spice Directory. But many are digestive remedies, such as aiding digestion and relieving flatulence, and these, in themselves, can keep the body healthy. There are other simple herbal remedies to try but, first, you will need to extract the active properties of the

RIGHT: Mace grows around nutmegs but the two spices are separated from each other soon after they are harvested. Mace has similar, more subtle properties to nutmeg.

spices. There are several ways to do this; the following three are the easiest to do at home.

INFUSIONS

These are also sometimes known as herbal teas, or *tisanes*, and are usually used for the soft leaves, stems or flowers of plants, rather than for dried spices, which are normally decocted.

DECOCTIONS

A decoction isolates the active properties from the hard parts of plants, such as bark and roots, and is a useful method for spices. Use 25g/1oz of whole spices to 900ml/ 1½ pints/3¾ cups of water in a pan. Bring to the boil and then leave to simmer for 15 minutes, until the liquid is reduced to 600ml/1pint/2½ cups.

INHALATIONS

Add about 300ml/½ pint/1¼ cups of an infusion or decoction to 600ml/1 pint/2½ cups of steaming water. Lean over the bowl, cover your head with a towel and inhale.

LEFT: Nutmeg stimulates the circulation and aids digestion.

AROMATHERAPY

Aromatherapy is the use of essential oils, extracted from plants either by distillation or by expression (squeezing). Essential oils are thought to contain the very essence of the plant's properties in a concentrated form, and so work in an efficient, yet natural and holistic way. Aromatherapy can be wonderfully relaxing, combining beauty treatments with remedial action. There are several ways to use essential oils, whose benefits are absorbed either through the skin or by inhalation. However, essential oils are very strong and only a very few drops should be used, so don't be tempted to use more than specified in recipes.

MASSAGE

Essential oils are strong and, with the exception of lavender and tea-tree oils, should never be used undiluted on the skin. Blend them with a base or carrier oil, such as sweet almond, wheatgerm or sunflower oil. Dilute them to 2.5% or 5 drops to every 10ml/2 tsp.

A skilled aromatherapist can encourage different oils to be absorbed into different parts of the body, to suit the patient's needs. Much of the benefit of aromatherapy massage is in relieving stress by the combination of massage and the relaxing properties of the essential oil.

Use chamomile for restlessness, eucalyptus for headaches, frankincense to soothe fear and anxiety, jasmine for stress, and lavender for insomnia, and insecurity.

IN AN AROMATIC BATH

Add a few drops of essential oil, blended with a base oil, to the bath either to invigorate you

LEFT: Burning an aromatic solution of a spice oil quickly scents the room and creates a relaxing ambience.

aroma of essential oils can have a beneficial effect, stimulating the olfactory nerve endings to work on the brain and so create a sense of well-being.

Remember never to leave the burner unattended, especially where there may be children in the house, and to top up the bowl with water as the liquid evaporates.

in the morning or to help you relax in the evening. This is a simple way for the skin to absorb the benefits of the essential oil.

IN A BURNER

Special aromatherapy burners consist of a shallow bowl over a small chamber containing a night-light. Almost fill the bowl with water and add a few drops of your chosen essential oil for a perfumed, relaxing ambience. According to aromatherapy theory, the

LEFT: Cloves are an antiseptic and can have a mild anaesthetic effect; oil of cloves was traditionally used to relieve toothache.

AS AN INHALATION

Add 6 drops of essential oil to a bowl of steaming water. Lean your head over the bowl, place a clean towel over your head and breathe deeply.

> *Caution*
>
> Spice oils, in particular, can be harsh and should be used with great care, especially in skin preparations. Cinnamon and clove oils should never be used on the skin at all. Do not attempt herbal or aromatherapy remedies if you are pregnant.

CHAPTER TWO

THE SPICE DIRECTORY

AND LUCENT SYROPS, TINCT WITH CINNAMON;

MANNA AND DATES, IN ARGOSY TRANSFERRED

FROM FEZ; AND SPICÈD DAINTIES, EVERY ONE,

FROM SILKEN SAMARCAND TO CEDARED LEBANON.

JOHN KEATS (1795–1821), THE EVE OF ST AGNES

ABOVE: Spices come from the roots, bark, flowers, seeds and fruits of many plants from many different parts of the world. Shown here are nutmeg (seeds), cloves (unopened flowers), mace (an arillus, or covering, surrounding the seed), and cinnamon (bark).

LEFT: Fragrant green cardamom, one of the most expensive spices, and red peppertree berries make a colourful combination.

The sheer diversity of spice sources is staggering, ranging from tiny fruits and seeds to the bark of large trees, roots, nuts, and even embryo seeds. The effect they must have on the quality of our lives can be gauged by the sheer determination man has put into discovering, cultivating and securing the trade of spices. There's always a fascinating story behind each and every spice.

BELOW: Delicate apricot-coloured mace, right, is the arilla that surrounds each nutmeg.

ALLSPICE BERRIES
Pimento officinalis

These peppercorn-like brown berries grow on leathery-leaved trees that grow to 9m/30ft. Allspice has a flavour which is a combination of cloves, cinnamon and nutmeg, which gives it its name. One of the few spices native to the western hemisphere, allspice grows profusely on the Caribbean island of Jamaica and, to a lesser extent, Central and parts of South America.

CULTIVATION Once the tree reaches maturity, at about four years old, flowers appear in June, July and August, which then quickly produce berries. These lose a lot of their volatile oil when they are ripe, so they are harvested as soon as they reach full size but before they are fully mature. Allspice is traditionally dried by spreading the stems out in the sun, but much is now dried in ovens.

CULINARY USES A pickling spice, used for fish and marinades and, in Jamaica, to flavour soups and stews.

MEDICINAL USES Relieves flatulence.

ANISE
Pimpinella anisum

The small, brownish-grey seeds of this annual plant, which reaches 60cm/2ft, have been prized since ancient Egyptian times for their mildly liquorice flavour. Native all around the Mediterranean (Egypt, Greece, Asia Minor), anise was cultivated in central Europe in the medieval period.

CULTIVATION Anise flowers by July and, as soon as the seeds have ripened in autumn, the plants are cut down. Commercially, the seeds are threshed out. Domestically, tie paper bags around the seed-heads and hang them up in a warm place to dry.

CULINARY USES Used to flavour pastis-type drinks, breads, cakes, curries and shellfish.

MEDICINAL USES Eases asthma, coughs and colic. Can help relieve flatulence.

BAY LEAVES
Laurus nobilis

These glossy leaves grow on an evergreen tree, which reaches a height of 7.5m/25ft in northern latitudes and up to 18m/60ft in warmer climates.

CULTIVATION Usually propagated from cuttings, this hardy tree flourishes with little attention in most temperate climates.

CULINARY USES A favourite flavouring worldwide, used for soups, sauces, stews, curries and desserts.

MEDICINAL USES Oil of bay can be used for sprains.

CARAWAY SEEDS
Carum carvi

The fruits of this plant (usually referred to as seeds) have been prized for centuries as a flavouring. The plant grows to about 60cm/2ft throughout the northern and central parts of Europe and Asia, India, North Africa, North America and Canada.

CULTIVATION Autumn-sown seeds ripen in August when the plants are cut down and the seeds threshed away. Traditionally sun-dried, they are nowadays more often oven-dried.

CULINARY USES Used in English cakes and biscuits (cookies), eastern-European vegetables, soups and stews.

MEDICINAL USES Eases colic, flatulence and bronchitis. Used for treating diarrhoea.

CARDAMOM PODS
Elettaria cardamomum

These green or brown pods are still one of the world's most expensive spices. Native to southern India and also grown in Sri Lanka, Thailand, Tanzania and Central America, the cardamom is a perennial plant that can grow to 5m/16ft.

CULTIVATION The harvest lasts three months, starting in October. Traditionally, the pods are dried on house roofs.

CULINARY USES A favourite flavouring for Indian dishes such as pilaus and biryanis as well as Persian recipes.

MEDICINAL USES Can be used to relieve painful colic and flatulence.

CASSIA BARK
Cinnamomum cassia/C. aromaticum

The coarse bark of a laurel-like tree, cassia is closely related to cinnamon, and is sometimes used as a substitute. Native to China and Vietnam, it is also cultivated in Sumatra, Sri Lanka, Japan, Java, Mexico and South America.

CULTIVATION Cultivated on plantations as coppices to encourage young shoots to grow from the roots. These are harvested and the bark is separated from the wood, which is burned.

CULINARY USES Used in cakes, sweets, puddings, curries and spicy casseroles.

MEDICINAL USES Often used to flavour unpleasant-tasting drugs, cassia bark also helps to relieve diarrhoea, nausea, vomiting and flatulence.

CAYENNE PEPPER
Capsicum frutescens

A type of chilli, grown in most tropical countries. It grows to 2m/6ft.

CULTIVATION Slender pods are harvested when red and ripe, then dried and ground to a fine powder.

CULINARY USES A spicy "pepper", used to flavour savoury dishes.

MEDICINAL USES Aids circulation, relieves chilblains, stimulates digestion.

CHILLI PEPPERS
Capsicum frutescens

Native to Central and South America, chillies now grow in many tropical and sub-tropical regions throughout the world. Fresh green chillies are the unripened fruits, which mature red, orange, yellow, brown or black, depending on the variety. *C. frutescens* is a perennial, growing to 60cm/2ft.

CULTIVATION Sown from seed, chillies need plenty of sun to ripen. Some are harvested while still green, others are allowed to ripen, and many of the red varieties are dried.

CULINARY USES One of the world's most popular spices, chillies are used to flavour hot dishes from Mexico, India, Japan, Indonesia and Africa.

MEDICINAL USES Chillies aid digestion and are good for improving circulation.

CINNAMON STICKS
Cinnamomum zeylanicum

Closely related to cassia, cinnamon is the bark of a laurel-like tree that grows up to 9m/30ft in Sri Lanka, India, China, Brazil and the West Indies.

CULTIVATION Cinnamon grows best in sand and needs plenty of rain and heat. The shoots are harvested and the inner bark is removed and dried for use.

CULINARY USES Cinnamon is a delicious fragrant flavouring for both sweets and savouries.

MEDICINAL USES Cinnamon relieves congestion, rheumatism, nausea, cramps and diarrhoea and stimulates circulation.

CLOVES
Eugenia caryophyllata

The unopened buds of a tropical evergreen that grows to 14m/45ft and is native to the Moluccan Islands (Spice Islands) in the southern Philippines. Cloves are now also grown in Mauritius, Brazil, and the East and West Indies.

CULTIVATION The trees fruit eight or nine years after planting. The whole tree is highly fragrant, but if the seeds are allowed to mature they lose their pungency, so the bud containing the embryo seed is harvested before it opens and is then dried. The best-quality cloves are marked as hand-picked.

CULINARY USES In sweet dishes and drinks as well as with meat, sauces and curries.

MEDICINAL USES Relieves indigestion; a whole clove can relieve toothache.

CORIANDER SEEDS
Coriandrum sativum

Dried seeds from a plant that resembles flat-leaved parsley and grows up to about 90cm/3ft. Native to southern Europe and the Middle East, it is also cultivated in India, South-east Asia and South America.

CULTIVATION Seeds can be sown outside in light, dry, warm soil in April, or under glass in March to be planted out in May. The seeds ripen in August, when the plant is cut down and the seeds threshed out.

CULINARY USES Coriander is one of the staple spices for Indian curries and is also used extensively in Middle Eastern, and southern-European flavourings for meat, fish and vegetables.

MEDICINAL USES Chiefly used to flavour other medicines.

CUMIN SEEDS
Cuminium cyminum

The seeds of an annual growing to about 25cm/10in and indigenous to Egypt, cumin is also cultivated in India, China and countries bordering the Mediterranean. There are black and "white" (actually brown) kinds.

CULTIVATION Although happiest in a hot climate, cumin can be grown in northern latitudes once all danger of frost is over and the soil is warm. When the seeds are nearly ripe, harvest the flowerheads, cover with paper bags and hang upside-down to collect the seeds.

CULINARY USES One of the main spices for Indian curries. Also used in the Middle East and North Africa to flavour vegetables, fish, lamb and chicken.

MEDICINAL USES Aids colic and digestion.

FENNEL SEEDS
Foenicularum vulgare

Seeds of a perennial plant growing to 2.5m/8ft. Indigenous to the Mediterranean, it spread to India in the east and into northern Europe to the west.

CULTIVATION Seeds are sown in well-drained soil in spring and harvested when ripe, in the autumn.

CULINARY USES The sweet, faintly aniseed flavour of fennel makes it perfect for fish, pork, soups and stocks.

MEDICINAL USES Fennel tea aids digestion and stimulates milk production in breast-feeding mothers.

FENUGREEK
Trigonella foenum-graecum

The seeds from the sickle-like pods of an annual herb that grows to about 60cm/24in high, native to the east of the Mediterranean, India, Egypt and Morocco. It can be grown in Great Britain. The name is derived from the Greek word for hay, as they used it to scent hay and flavour horse and cattle feed.

CULTIVATION Seeds are sown under glass in late spring or directly into the soil once the risk of frosts is over. Seedlings are thinned out and pods harvested when ripe.

CULINARY USES Used in curries, and as a flavouring in confectionery.

MEDICINAL USES A paste of seeds soaked in water was used in Egyptian times to prevent fevers and ease stomach pain. Poultices of fenugreek can be used on boils and spots.

GINGER
Zingiber officinale

The rhizome (underground stem) of a reed-like perennial grown in South-east Asia, India and China. Sold fresh, dried or powdered it is called root ginger; the same part of the plant, preserved in syrup, is known as stem ginger.

CULTIVATION Ginger root is harvested annually and part of this is re-planted to provide the next crop, about ten months later. Grown at home in a pot, parts of the rhizome can simply be broken off as needed.

CULINARY USES Ginger is a favourite flavouring in Asian cooking, with meat, fish and vegetables. It is also used to flavour pickles, chutneys, cakes and biscuits (cookies).

MEDICINAL USES Relieves travel and pregnancy sickness, helps circulation and also soothes chilblains.

JUNIPER BERRIES
Juniperis communis

These are blue-black berries that are produced only by female bushes of a small evergreen that grows to about 2m/6ft, native to Europe, North Africa, northern Asia and North America.

CULTIVATION Plantations need to include male as well as female bushes. The berries take two to three years to ripen, so both unripe green and blue berries appear at the same time. The berries are hand-picked and laid out on shelves to dry.

CULINARY USES Used for cooking game, pâtés and red cabbage and, commercially, to flavour gin.

MEDICINAL USES Juniper relieves diseases of the kidney and bladder and is used as a diuretic.

LEMONGRASS
Cymbopogon citratus

A spring-onion-like perennial plant with dry, grass-like leaves; it grows in South-east Asia, Central and South America and the West Indies.

CULTIVATION Lemongrass requires a tropical climate with plenty of water and sunshine. Can be propagated by division.

CULINARY USES The delicate lemon flavouring, with a hint of ginger, is a favourite of Asian cuisine, being used with fish, chicken and vegetables.

MEDICINAL USES Lemongrass eases sore throats and respiratory problems and helps to clear oily skin. A few drops of the essential oil, which is antiseptic and antifungal, has sedative and deodorizing effects in the bath.

MACE
Myristica fragrans

The lace-like covering of nutmeg, which is the seed of an evergreen tree that is native to the Moluccas, New Guinea and the West Indies.

CULTIVATION Only the female bears fruit, which look like golden pears. They take up to nine years to mature but then produce up to 2,000 nutmegs a year. The fruits split open when ripe, revealing the nutmeg and scarlet mace. The mace and nutmegs are separated out and the mace dried.

CULINARY USES Mace's subtle flavour is a perfect addition to sauces, desserts, white meats and fish dishes.

MEDICINAL USES Mace aids digestion and circulation. In the past, it was used in the treatment of fevers.

MUSTARD SEEDS
Brassica alba, B. nigra

Black or white small, round seeds from the pods of an annual, probably a native of the Mediterranean but also growing in the rest of Europe, Canada and North America. The black variety is normally found in southern Italy and Ethiopia.

CULTIVATION Seeds are sown in spring and harvested in late summer when they are almost ripe. They dry in the pods.

CULINARY USES Mustard is the main ingredient for mustard relish, and mustard seeds are used whole in Indian dishes.

MEDICINAL USES Both kinds of mustard seeds have been used as laxatives. Infusions can be used to relieve sore throats, bronchitis and rheumatism.

NUTMEG
Myristica fragrans

The nut of a peach-like tree that reaches about 7m/25ft high, native to the Malaysian peninsula and Moluccan Islands and cultivated in Sumatra.

CULTIVATION The female tree is about nine years old before it fruits but will then produce nutmegs for about 75 years, with up to three harvests a year. After harvesting the nutmegs are dried separately from the mace, a process that can take up to six weeks.

CULINARY USES A delicious, mellow spice that can be used in drinks, sweets, puddings and savouries.

MEDICINAL USES As an essential oil used in aromatherapy, nutmeg stimulates the circulation and heartbeat.

PAPRIKA
Capsicum annuum

The powdered spice made by grinding dried peppers (bell peppers), which grow on an annual plant that reaches 150cm/5ft. Native to South America, it is now also widely grown in southern Europe and the southern states of North America. Can be grown further north under glass.

CULTIVATION Seeds are sown under glass in early spring and planted out once there is no danger of frost and the earth is warm. The peppers are ready to harvest in late summer. They are then dried and ground.

CULINARY USES Paprika is usually mild, though, depending on the variety, it can be hot, too. It is used in Hungarian goulash, vegetables, fish dishes and cream sauces.

MEDICINAL USES None known.

PEPPERCORNS
Piper nigrum

The dried fruit of a climbing plant that can reach up to 6m/20ft but, commercially, is allowed to reach only 2m/6ft. Native to southern India and Vietnam, now also grown in Malaysia, Malabar and the West Indies.

CULTIVATION The plants produce fruits from about four years after planting. For black pepper, the peppercorns are harvested just as they begin to turn red, but before they are fully ripe, and then they are dried in the sun. For white pepper, they are allowed to ripen and the outer skins removed before drying. Green peppercorns are unripe peppercorns.

CULINARY USES Pepper enlivens almost all savoury dishes and is a staple condiment.

MEDICINAL USES Aids digestion and relieves constipation, flatulence and arthritis.

POPPY SEEDS
Papaver somniferum

The seeds from the opium poppy, an annual that grows to 120cm/4ft in China, South-east Asia, India and the Middle East.

CULTIVATION It is illegal to grow the opium poppy in Britain or the United States. Where it is cultivated, the seeds are sown in March or April. After the flowers have bloomed and petals fallen, the seed-heads are bent down until they are firm, around September. The seed-heads hold the milky juice, which is used for opium, as well as the seeds, which are not narcotic.

CULINARY USES Used to coat breads and in noodle dishes. Used in Indian pancakes such as chapattis.

MEDICINAL USES None known.

SAFFRON
Crocus sativus

The stigmas of autumn crocuses growing to 15cm/6in, probably native to Greece and the eastern Mediterranean, saffron also grows in Spain, India, Turkey and China.

CULTIVATION Corms are planted 15cm/6in apart in July and the three stigmas in each flower are harvested and dried in September.

CULINARY USES About 40,000 stigmas are needed to make 1kg/2lb saffron, making this an extremely expensive spice, which lends a honey-like flavour and bright yellow colouring to many rice dishes in India, the Middle East and Mediterranean. In England, it is traditionally used in cakes and buns.

MEDICINAL USES Saffron was used in the past to treat haemorrhage of the uterus.

SESAME SEEDS
Sesamum indicum

Creamy-white seeds from the pods of an annual plant growing to 2m/6ft. Indigenous to India, it is now also grown in much of Asia, Mexico and the southern United States.

CULTIVATION Sesame is grown from seed, and harvested about six months later.

CULINARY USES The main ingredient for tahini paste, a popular flavouring in the Middle East and the one that gives hummus its distinctive character. Sesame seeds are used in many Chinese, Japanese, Korean and Indian recipes, as part of the masala or spice paste, and in Britain to garnish breads.

MEDICINAL USES None known.

STAR ANISE
Illicium verum

The pretty, star-shaped fruit of an evergreen from the magnolia family, native to China and South east Asia.

CULTIVATION The star-shaped fruits are picked off the trees, which reach 8m/26ft, before they are ripe. They are then dried in the sun.

CULINARY USES This is a popular oriental spice, being one of the constituents of five-spice powder. In the west, it is sometimes used in pickles and relishes.

MEDICINAL USES None known.

TURMERIC
Curcuma longa

The root of a tropical perennial that grows to 1m/3ft and is native to South-east Asia, it is also grown in India, China, Australia, Africa, Peru and the West Indies.

CULTIVATION When the rhizomes are harvested, small parts are replaced in the ground to provide the next crop.

CULINARY USES Most often presented as a bright yellow powder, turmeric is used extensively in India, the Middle East and North Africa for curries, sauces and rice dishes.

MEDICINAL USES Turmeric is used more as a colouring than for therapeutic purposes in medicines.

VANILLA PODS
Vanilla plenifolia fragrans

The pod of an orchid native to Mexico and Central America, vanilla also grows in Madagascar, the Seychelles and Tahiti.

CULTIVATION Trained up posts on plantations, each flower blooms for only a day, so they are artificially fertilized, after which the pods take nine months to mature. They are still green when they are picked and then there is a six-month drying process, by which time the pods have their familiar, dark-brown colouring.

CULINARY USES Vanilla is the classic flavouring for ice creams, cakes, desserts and confectionery, particularly in partnership with chocolate.

MEDICINAL USES Vanilla is used to perfume cosmetics.

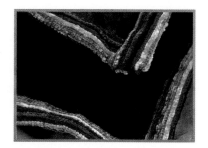

CHAPTER THREE

$\mathscr{D}$ECORATING WITH $\mathscr{S}$PICES

THE HERBS WERE SPRINGING IN THE VALE

GREEN GINGER PLANTS AND LICORICE PALE

AND CLOVES THEIR SWEETNESS OFFER

WITH NUTMEGS, TOO, TO PUT TO ALE

NO MATTER WHETHER FRESH OR STALE

OR ELSE KEEP IN THE COFFER.

GEOFFREY CHAUCER (1340–1400)

ABOVE: Add cloves or cassia bark to the filling of velvet cushions for sumptuous, aromatic furnishings.

LEFT: Deliciously aromatic, spices can be used to make a surprisingly strong impact all around the home. This table, for example, has been laid with tablemats made only of cinnamon sticks woven with raffia.

The dictionary definition of spices – the dried aromatic parts of plants – suggests little of their decorative qualities. In reality, however, the colours and textures of spices offer plenty of scope for making decorative items for the home while, at the same time, lending an evocative, exotic fragrance.

Spices come in a glorious palette of natural colours, from deep red chillies or warm, golden turmeric, through terracotta-coloured cinnamon, and the earthy shades of nutmeg, cloves and pepper, to the subtle greens of cardamom and fennel. Their shapes and textures, too, provide plenty of variety, from the fine-grained seeds of cumin, coriander and sesame to spiky star anise or pencil-proportioned cinnamon quills, oval nutmegs and the generous spheres of dried oranges.

There is something beguiling about beautiful gifts which have the added dimension of aroma. Cushions can be filled with cloves or cinnamon; throws and lampshades can be fringed with nutmegs; dramatic topiaries and wreaths made from a range of

RIGHT: A simple wreath packed with small chillies makes a wonderfully textural wall or window decoration.

ABOVE: The subtle tones of dried oranges look wonderful with old copper.

spices will impart a lovely, exotic fragrance all around your home.

This chapter covers items that will create an impact in your home, and so these are the largest projects. Some use generous quantities of materials and it is important to make sure you have enough before you start. Don't be put off, though, because many of these storecupboard standbys are not costly and plenty of material does not necessarily make a project expensive. Cloves, for example, are relatively cheap; though for convenience' sake, simply to get the bulk you need, it is best to buy in large quantities. Either track down the wholesalers and buy by the kilo or

pound, or search out Asian supermarkets. Some of the materials used in the projects are best bought from dried-flower suppliers, who sell certain spices for their looks, rather than their flavour. This is the best source for cinnamon sticks, for example, which are available in a choice of lengths and usually come in bags that contain quills of a uniform width. You'll also find a wide choice of chillies from dried-flower suppliers, ranging from pencil-thin ones to those that are large, fleshy and ruby-toned. Ask, too, for boxes of hand-picked cloves, star anise and reindeer moss, which make excellent filling material and are complementary in colour to many spices. And, of course, the florist or dried-flower supplier is the best source for dry florist's foam base shapes.

If you do buy spices from florists, bear in mind that they have not necessarily been prepared in hygienic conditions for consumption, and should be kept well away from the storecupboard. When working with chillies, it is best to wear thin surgical gloves (look for them in the chemist [drugstore]); otherwise, wash your hands scrupulously with washing-up liquid (soap) afterwards, as their juices penetrate the skin and can burn if you later touch the

more sensitive skin on the face or near the eyes.

Spices are lovely to work with, exuding their delicious aroma as you fashion them into beautiful pieces; some, like cloves, also release their precious oils, which leave your hands beautifully soft. None of these projects are difficult to do and, when they're finished, you'll be rewarded with dramatic, aromatic decorations for your home.

BELOW: The soft greens of cardamom pods are decorative in themselves. Pile them into a green vase for a sweetly scented room freshener.

NUTMEG LAMPSHADE

A nutmeg fringe lends wit and charm to a simple parchment lampshade. Once finished, team it with an Indian carved wooden lamp, such as this, or, for a completely different and more modern look, fix it on to a metal tablelamp.

MATERIALS

lampshade, with cord thonging if possible
pencil and single hole punch, if necessary
tape measure
about 60 nutmegs (for a 35cm/14in diameter shade)
12m/13yd rayon ribbon, about 3mm/⅛ in wide
scissors
all-purpose glue
large-eyed needle

1 If the lampshade does not already have holes, mark the positions for holes evenly spaced about 2cm/¾ in apart around the bottom of the shade, then make the holes using a single hole punch. For each hole, you will need one nutmeg and one length of ribbon 18cm/7in long. Start by cutting one length of ribbon 18cm/7in long. Lay it on a flat surface and, starting about 4cm/1½ in from one end, carefully apply a 7.5cm/3in line of glue.

LEFT: The varying sizes of nutmegs add to the overall natural charm of the fringing.

2 Place a nutmeg lengthways on the ribbon and tie the two ends at the top of the nutmeg in a reef knot. One end will be longer than the other. Repeat with all the other nutmegs.

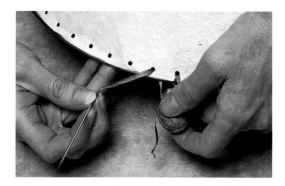

3 If your lampshade has cord thonging, remove most of this from the bottom of the lampshade. Thread the long end of the ribbon through the needle and pass this through one of the holes, from behind.

4 Bring the needle around the outside of the lampshade and back through the hole from behind again. Remove the needle.

5 Bring the short end of the ribbon up to meet the long end and tie together in a tight, neat reef knot. Repeat with all nutmegs. Trim the ends using sharp scissors. At the top circumference of the lampshade, remove the original thonging and replace it with matching ribbon.

EVERLASTING MIXED-SPICE WREATH

The glorious, rich colours and robust textures of the larger spices make them ideal raw materials for an exotic aromatic wreath that could adorn a wall for years to come. Leave them natural or rub on a little gilt for a touch of sparkle.

MATERIALS
picture framer's gilt wax (optional)
17 small dried oranges
18 × 5cm/2in cinnamon sticks
raffia
scissors
glue gun and hot wax glue
2 large handfuls dried mace
willow wreath, about 30cm/12in diameter
about 80 nutmegs

1 Rub a light veil of picture framer's gilt on to the oranges, for a richer finished effect, if you like.

2 Tie the cinnamon lengths into bundles of three, using raffia, and trim the ends. If you like, you can rub gilt wax along some of the sticks to provide highlights.

LEFT: Gilding the oranges increases the richness of the look.

3 Using the glue gun, fix a layer of the dried mace on to the wreath to provide a spicy base.

4 In the same way, fix the cinnamon bundles on at equal intervals. These will section off the wreath, providing a framework for the rest of the design.

5 Fix about three oranges randomly in each section of wreath, between two cinnamon bundles.

6 Glue nutmegs on the wreath to fill in between the cinnamon bundles and oranges; add more to the inside edge of the wreath, to give greater depth.

AROMATIC TABLEMATS

Stunning in their simplicity, these cinnamon tablemats could not be easier to do. When finished, they're not only pleasing to the eye: when you put hot plates on them, they release a subtle, delicious aroma.

<u>MATERIALS FOR EACH MAT</u>

about 22 slim cinnamon sticks, about
18cm/7in long
secateurs
natural raffia

❧*1* Cut the cinnamon sticks to length, if necessary, using secateurs, and then arrange them on a flat surface, side by side. You may need to twist them so they lie together snugly, without large gaps. Fold a length of raffia in half and loop the fold over the top of the end cinnamon stick, ready to begin weaving.

❧*2* Bring the lower piece of raffia up, and the upper piece down, and then slip the next cinnamon stick in between the two pieces of raffia.

❧*3* Repeat until all the sticks have been woven in. When you reach the last stick tie the ends of the raffia.

RIGHT: Dried-flower suppliers sell cinnamon sticks in various, ready-trimmed, sizes.

❧*4* Turn the mat round and tie the raffia at the other end of the cinnamon sticks.

SPICY SAMPLER

Create a delicate sampler by trapping spice seedcases between translucent fabric and sandwiching it between two layers of glass, to give a floating effect.

MATERIALS
0.5m/¹/2 yd fine open-mesh fabric,
e.g. cesu organza
tape measure
scissors
needle and dressmaker's pins
matching sewing thread
handful each of miniature dried chillies,
cumin seeds, cardamom pods and coriander seeds
matching or contrasting stranded
embroidery thread
picture frame, about 45 × 35cm/18 × 14in,
preferably with glass back
0.5m/¹/2 yd gold polyester organza

1 ✥ Cut two pieces of fabric about 25 × 25cm/10 × 10in. Lay one on top of the other and then use pins to mark a 15cm/6in square in the middle of the fabric. Work a line of stitches along three sides of the square, between the pins. Work two more parallel vertical lines, 5cm/2in apart, from the bottom of the square, level with the outside stitching lines. This will give you three vertical channels. Place chillies in one channel, cumin seeds in another and cardamom pods in the third, to a depth of almost 5cm/2in, and then run a line of tacking (basting) along the top of these. Stitch just above the tacking (basting).

LEFT: This sampler is made up of just four different spices, arranged checkerboard fashion.

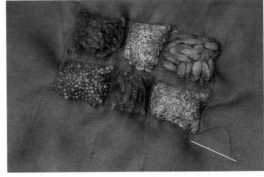

2 ✥ Repeat with a second row, filling the channels with coriander seeds, chillies and cumin seeds, and a third row using cardamom, coriander seeds and chillies. Stitch the top of the square.

3 ✥ "Embroider" over the stitching to give a richer finished effect. Do this by working running stitch using three strands of stranded embroidery thread in a matching or contrasting colour.

4 Trim the top square so it is a little smaller than the underneath square. Fray all the ends, to give a feathery effect.

5 Put the sampler in the frame, face-down on the front glass. Cut the gold polyester organza to size and place it over the frame, as backing. Put the backing glass on top and clip the glass into place. The finished piece can be mounted in any frame, but it retains its transparent quality if it is mounted in a frame which has glass front and back. This frame was found in a high street interior shop. Hang the piece so that it catches the light and lends a floating look to the sampler.

FRAGRANT SPICE CUSHION

There's something gloriously sensuous about this taffeta cushion. The cardamom and fennel filling, trapped behind a translucent mesh fabric, offers texture and movement as well as fragrance. The large golden tassels add yet more movement.

MATERIALS
35cm/14in square toning cesu organza
35cm/14in square cinnamon-coloured taffeta
dressmaker's pins
needle and tacking (basting) thread
tape measure
scissors
4 large handfuls cardamom pods
½ handful fennel seeds (optional)
4 gold tassels about 10cm/4in long
1.5m/1½ yd ribbon, 7cm/2¾ in wide

1 With wrong sides together, pin the organza to the taffeta. Turn in the edges all round. Pin and tack (baste). Stitch through all layers, leaving a 10cm/4in gap for the filling. Measure 7cm/2¾ in (or the width of your chosen ribbon) in from each side of the cushion and mark with pins at each corner as guides for stitching the cushion seams to the correct distance from the edge.

2 Leave a gap in the stitching corresponding with the gap in the first row of stitches, for the filling. Fill the middle section of the cushion with cardamom pods or a cardamom and fennel mixture.

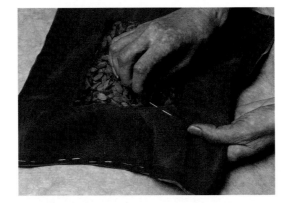

3 Stitch to close. Turn in and pin the outside edges of the gap and stitch to close and neaten. Stitch a tassel to each corner, on the upper side.

4 Cut two lengths of ribbon to a little longer than the width of the cushion. Fold down the corner of each and crease firmly, to create a mitre line. Stitch along this line and trim off near the line of stitching. Put the ribbon over the organza and, using hemming stitch, carefully stitch the ribbon to the outside edges of two sides of the cushion.

5 Mitre the next two corners in the same way and stitch these two sides down. Mitre the last corner and stitch that down. Finally, hem the inside edge of the ribbon close to the cardamom-filled section.

AROMATIC CLOVE CUSHION

Sumptuous clove-filled velvet cushions instantly lend a romantic and fragrant decorative touch to any bedroom. Cassia bark would make for a more moody and exotic alternative filling.

MATERIALS
dressmaker's scissors
0.5m/¹/₂ yd heavyweight wadding (batting)
tape measure
needle and matching sewing threads
about 150g/6oz cloves
0.5m/¹/₂ yd dress velvet
2m/2¹/₄ yd chenille braid or similar,
7.5cm/3in wide
dressmaker's pins
cushion pad

2 Cut two pieces of velvet, each 30 × 45cm/12 × 18in; two pieces of braid 40cm/16in long and two 50cm/20in long. Lay one velvet cushion piece on a flat surface, right-side up. Fold the two longer pieces of braid in half, wrong sides together, and put them on top of the velvet, with the braid's selvedges matching the long edges of the velvet. Pin.

4 Turn right-sides out and put one of the short pieces of braid, right-side down, along one end of the cushion, matching selvedges and raw edges. Stitch, taking in both thicknesses of velvet. Trim the seam. Turn the braid over to the other side of the cushion. Turn the ends in and slip-stitch to close; neatly stitch the braid in position along its length.

1 Cut a piece of wadding (batting) 55 × 40cm/22 × 16in and fold in half. Stitch together, fill with cloves and stitch to close.

3 Put the second piece of velvet right-side down on top, matching the edges. Pin and stitch along the length of both seams.

5 Put the clove-filled pad and cushion pad into the velvet cover and then apply the braid to the open end, following step 4.

SPICY OBELISK

It is easy to create impact, simply by thinking big. This most elegant obelisk evokes eighteenth-century splendour, yet it is incredibly easy to make. The combination of cloves and star anise makes a pretty and rich texture, set off by rich turquoise ribbon – a favourite Regency colour.

MATERIALS
knife
dry florist's foam cone, about 30cm/12in diameter
metal urn, about 30cm/12in diameter
dressmaker's pins
2m/2¼ yd wire-edged ribbon, about 5cm/2in wide
wire cutters
florist's reel wire
60 star anise
1 kg/2lb cloves, hand-picked, if possible

RIGHT: The star anise gives a pretty effect, though, since many stars in each packet will be broken, you will have to buy plenty of them. If this proves a problem, an all-clove and ribbon obelisk would still retain the same striking elegance.

1 Using the knife, trim the florist's foam cone so it fits snugly into the urn.

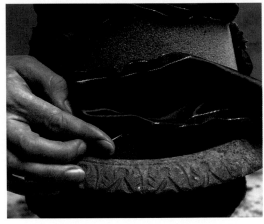

2 Use the pins to fix the ribbon to the cone, starting at the bottom, working around the top and then down again. Scrunch the ribbon as you go.

3 Cut two lengths of florist's wire about 5cm/2in long for each star anise. Place them over the star, forming a cross on the top, then twist the ends together at the back.

4 Use the wire to fix the star anise to the cone, creating a pleasing pattern.

5 Stud the rest of the cone with cloves, filling it well so no foam shows. Work in rows, to create a neat finished effect.

MOPHEAD CHILLI TOPIARY

Mophead faux trees make fabulous fireplace ornaments, either on the mantelpiece, as here, or standing on the hearth. Make them large for greater impact.

MATERIALS FOR EACH TREE
knife
dry florist's foam bricks, to fill the container
container, about 20cm/8in diameter
2 pieces contorted willow, each 50cm/20in long
medium-gauge florist's reel wire
1 kg/2lb large dried red chillies
dry florist's foam ball about 20cm/8in diameter
handful reindeer moss
short florist's stub wires, bent into "hairpin" shapes

ABOVE: Gold and black lacquer-style containers complement the exotic look of the trees.

1 Using the knife, cut the bricks of foam to fit snugly into the container. Entwine the two pieces of willow and fix them into the foam, in the container.

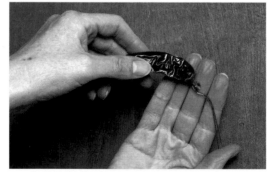

2 Cut a length of wire and wrap it around the stalk end of a chilli. Twist the two ends together and trim to 2.5cm/1in. Trim the stalk close to the wire. Repeat with the other chillies.

3 Fix the foam ball to the top of the willow and fix a circle of chillies into this.

4 Fill in one half of the foam ball with chillies, row by row, and then fill in the other side. Dress the top of the foam with moss, fixing it into place with wires.

NUTMEG-FRINGED THROW

Fabulously fringed with nutmeg and chenille, here's a throw that can be used as a decorative overcloth, or on a bed or sofa. The same technique can be used to give ordinary curtains a very special trimming.

MATERIALS
nutmegs (allow 1 per 4cm/1¹/₂ in of border)
1 ball chunky mustard-coloured chenille
tape measure
scissors
all-purpose glue
large-eyed needle
turmeric-coloured throw

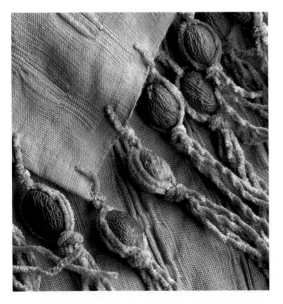

1 For each nutmeg, cut one length of chenille about 15cm/6in long and one about 70cm/28in. Fold the long piece in half and half again and put the short one through the top loop. The nutmeg will be glued at the top of the loop, trapping the short piece of chenille which will be used to sew the nutmeg fringe to the throw. The first step towards this aim is to make a line of glue lengthways around the nutmeg.

LEFT: Once completed, the nutmeg and chenille fringing is surprisingly robust, though it would not stand up to machine washing. Instead, rinse it through by hand in warm water.

2 Put the nutmeg at the top of the loop of the doubled-over chenille and then tie a knot in the loose ends, close to the bottom of the nutmeg.

3 With the same nutmeg, gather together the two ends of the short piece of chenille and tie them together in a knot near the top of the nutmeg.

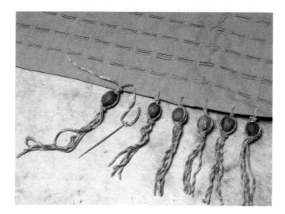

4 Thread one of the short ends into the needle and pass it through from the front to the back of the throw, at one corner. Pass the other loose end to the back and tie the two ends together in a reef knot, at the back of the throw. Repeat with another nutmeg, placing it 4cm/1½ in away from the first one. Continue, either down only two opposite sides of the throw, or on all four sides. Trim the chenille at the back of the throw, close to the knots. Trim the long ends of the fringe so they are even.

CINNAMON PICTURE FRAME

Quills of cinnamon can be pieced together on a picture frame, to transform a cheap pine original into one that is far more substantial, with a rich, textured look. The end result is wonderfully aromatic.

MATERIALS
secateurs
enough cinnamon sticks to cover the frame,
4 to a width
pine picture frame
glue gun and hot wax glue

1 Using secateurs, cut the cinnamon sticks into 5cm/2in lengths.

2 Starting at one corner of the frame, glue the first stick at the outside edge, so it projects proud of the corner. Put the next one at right angles to it, so it butts up against the first. Put the third stick next to the first, so it butts up against the second. Continue around the frame, creating a brick-laid effect the width of two sticks.

3 Now make a row in a similar way to the inside of the original inside row and another row to the outside of the original outside row.

4 If there are little spaces between some of the cinnamon sticks, fix small pieces of cinnamon into the gaps, until none of the pine is visible.

NUTMEG AND CINNAMON HEART

The subtle shades and gentle aromas of nutmeg and cinnamon make this a perfect decorative hanging or table ornament.

MATERIALS
knife
1 dry florist's foam brick
heart-shaped copper cake tin, about
30cm/12in diameter
about 400 cinnamon sticks, 7.5cm/3in long
secateurs
glue gun and hot wax glue
50 nutmegs
pencil
handful reindeer moss

1 Cut three strips of foam, each about 5cm/2in wide and the depth of the cake tin. Position them lengthways in the heart, with one in the middle and one each half way between the middle and the outside edge. Trim the ends to fit.

2 If you have fewer, longer cinnamon sticks, cut them to length using secateurs. Adjust the length a little, if necessary, to create two or three equal lengths from each stick, depending on the length you buy, but make sure they will project above the rim of the container by about 2.5cm/1in. Fit the foam strips in position. These will provide the base for the nutmeg stripes. Place the cinnamon sticks upright all around the outside edge and between the foam strips. Pack the sticks in tightly, until they are very firmly wedged.

LEFT: This burnished copper container perfectly complements the natural spice shades of its contents.

3 Apply a little glue to the bottom of each nutmeg and fix them in rows on to the foam.

4 Using the end of a pencil, gently poke a little moss between each nutmeg to cover any foam.

CHAPTER FOUR

AROMATIC
DETAILS

I HAVE COVERED MY BED WITH COLOURED LINENS

FROM EGYPT. I HAVE PERFUMED MY BED WITH MYRRH,

ALOES AND CINNAMON.

PROVERBS 7:16,17

ABOVE: Citrus and bay leaves provide a base for a long-lasting
Christmas garland.

LEFT: Aromatic details add a subtle yet spicy touch to the home. Use spices
for simple celebration decorations, or for something more permanent, such
as a sweet-scented tablecentre.

Just as a pinch of spice can transform a simple dish into something far more exotic, so even a few unusual touches can add piquancy to your home. Whatever you make using spices will give off a fragrant aroma, so that any decorative object becomes a natural room freshener too.

In this chapter, there is a wealth of quick ideas for spicing up all the rooms in your home. If you have a limited amount of time but want to add something special to an occasion you will find the perfect idea here. Many parties, evening dinners or Christmas celebrations are made perfect by thoughtful

LEFT: The natural tones of raffia and cinnamon are always pleasing together.

finishing touches. A room lit by scented candles, charming napkin decorations, or a delicious spicy-scented tablecentre will make your family and friends feel cherished and welcomed. The ideas in this chapter include small topiaries that can be used as tablecentres, or to decorate shelves or mantels; table-accessory ideas to add a touch of the exotic to special-occasion meals; there are easy-to-make festive decorations and garlands to add spice to special celebrations. Finally, there's a giftwrap idea.

One of the problems of learning a new craft is simply getting to know how to handle the materials and knowing how to create the desired finished effect. And, although spices are not difficult to handle, even for beginners, it is not until you start putting cloves into foam, for example, that you can work out just how close they need to be, or how tightly (or loosely) to fill something with cardamom pods. Most of the ideas in this

LEFT: The rich, ruby tones of chillies provide vibrant colour that adds an exotic touch.

chapter are fairly small, simple and quick to do. The investment in terms of time and even money is not large, yet the end results are brilliant. Some are so easy, the children will enjoy joining in. Offer them one of the smaller topiaries, such as the spice cone, pink

BELOW: Dried spices threaded on to raffia make witty curtain tie backs. Here, cinnamon sticks, bay leaves and chillies have been used.

ABOVE: Star anise is so pretty, all you need to do is put a few handfuls in a copper bowl for an unusual, aromatic accessory.

peppercorn urn or Cinnamon and Peppertree Berry Pot for starters. Even six-year-olds can be delighted with the results. A word of warning, though: give them all-purpose glue to use, rather than a hot wax glue, which, if the glue it contains touches their skin, would burn painfully.

Whatever your crafting skills, all these ideas are easy and fun to do with most satisfying end results for delightful details that can transform your home and make an event into a really special occasion.

MINI SPICE TOPIARIES

The diminutive size of many spices means they make perfect raw materials for scaled-down topiaries. Quick and easy to do, you can soon create a whole range of charming natural accessories for every room in the house. These little trees also make delightful gifts. Geometric shapes – cones, orbs, even pillars – always look smart, echoing the original garden topiary shapes of clipped box from seventeenth-century formal gardens.

RIGHT AND BELOW: Pink peppercorns make witty material for miniature metal urns. Spilling over the rim, they give a very voluptuous feel. Simply secure a small dry florist's foam ball in the urn and then glue on the peppercorns, using a glue gun and hot wax glue.

RIGHT AND ABOVE: A small florist's foam cone makes the base for this delightful clove and star anise topiary. Shave the foam at the base, to fit the pot, then trim the top to the desired shape. The wired star anise are put in first, then the cloves. The all-natural colours and materials of this piece make a pleasing and timeless combination.

SCENTED NAPKIN RINGS

Inspired by hair "scrunchies", these cardamom-filled organza napkin rings make elegant, yet inexpensive, table accessories. Cardamom is a perfect spice for the filling, as it has a fresh, sweet perfume that won't overwhelm the aroma of the food.

MATERIALS FOR SIX NAPKIN RINGS

scissors

0.5m/1½ yd metal-shot organza

tape measure

1m/1yd elastic

needle and matching thread

bodkin or safety pin

6 handfuls cardamom pods

BELOW: Tuck a few cinnamon sticks into the rings for extra spice.

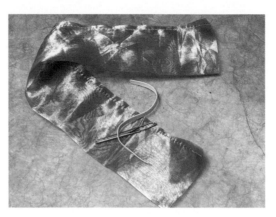

1 For each ring, cut a piece of organza 46 × 15cm/18 × 6in and a piece of elastic 15cm/6in long. Fold the organza strip, right-sides together, in half lengthways. Stitch the long side.

2 Use the bodkin or safety pin to thread the elastic through the organza tube and stitch the two ends of elastic together.

3 Turn the fabric through right-sides out. Loosely fill the scrunchie with cardamom pods.

4 Turn in the raw ends and then slip-stitch the two ends of the organza tube together to close. Make sure you start by matching the seams at the join.

SPICY TABLECENTRE

The glorious tones and aromas of spices add up to an exquisite tablecentre, exciting the taste buds, even before the meal is served. The rich lustre of the copper bowl lends an eastern influence.

MATERIALS

strip of gold-shot organza, 15cm × 1.25m/
6 × 50in or enough to fit loosely around the top of
the bowl
1.5m/1½ yd green ribbon, about 4cm/1½ in wide
dressmaker's pins
glue gun and hot wax glue
copper bowl, about 25cm/10in diameter
2 sheets newspaper
4 handfuls dried mace
6 limes
5 pomanders or dried oranges
4 sprigs fresh bay leaves

1 Fold the strip of organza loosely in half lengthways. Join the end of the organza tube and the ribbon with a pin and then twist them together along their length. Pin them together at the other end.

2 Using the glue gun, fix the ribbon and organza strip around the top of the bowl, loosely garlanding it as you go.

LEFT: A quick and easy tablecentre.

3 Fill the bottom of the bowl with scrunched-up newspaper and then completely cover this with the mace, so it comes to about 2.5cm/1in below the rim of the bowl.

4 Add a layer of limes. Pile on the pomanders and then finish with bay leaves.

STARRY SPICE GIFTWRAP

Gold tissue, cellophane and gilded star anise make for extremely elegant giftwrap, which can be used for even awkwardly shaped gifts. Tissue easily takes to any form and the cellophane "overwrap" allows space for curves, corners and points.

MATERIALS
gold tissue paper
cellophane
gold cord
picture framer's gilt wax
about 12 star anise (depending on size of parcel)
glue gun and hot wax glue

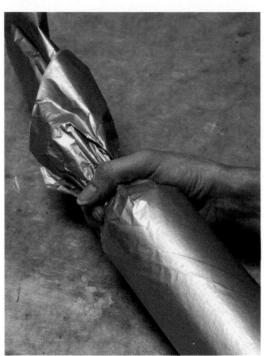

1 Wrap the gift in gold tissue. This bottle has a cracker-style end; a square or rectangular parcel could be completely wrapped in the normal way.

LEFT: Star anise adds a spicy, decorative touch. Gild each one for a festive look.

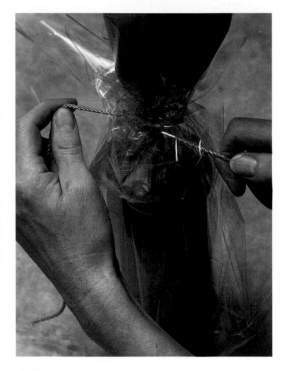

2 Cut enough cellophane to over-wrap the parcel loosely and tie it at the top with gold cord. To wrap this bottle, the four corners have been pulled up and tied in. The edges of the cellophane did not fit under the cord, but projected out, forming elegant wings.

3 Rub picture framer's gilt wax on to the star anise with your finger.

4 Using the glue gun, fix the star anise in position, placing them at intervals to create a pleasing overall effect.

BAY AND ORANGE GARLAND

The warm tones of dried orange slices, nestled in glossy evergreen bay leaves, make a glorious Christmas garland. It is very simple to do and, if you have a bay tree that needs pruning, inexpensive.

MATERIALS
florist's garland base or chicken wire and
florist's foam
wire cutters
2 florist's foam bricks
knife
secateurs
about 200 fresh bay leaves per 30cm/12in
of garland
florist's reel wire
1 pack dried orange or lemon slices
wire-edged ribbon, about twice as long as
the mantel

1 If you cannot find a garland base, make your own with chicken wire as follows. Cut a piece of chicken wire the length of the mantel and 15cm/6in wide. Lay soaked and cut lengths of florist's foam along the length of the chicken wire. Roll up the chicken wire to make a long, foam-filled sausage and tuck in the sharp wire ends. Soak the florist's foam bricks in water and then cut them up and put them in the garland base. Using the secateurs, trim sprigs of bay leaves off the branch and fix them into the garland base, until it is completely covered.

LEFT: Wire up the orange slices in pairs, to give extra colour impact.

2 Cut 20cm/8in lengths of florist's wire. Wire the citrus slices in pairs, twisting the ends together.

3 Fix the wired citrus slices into the garland, then wind the ribbon along its whole length.

SIMPLE SPICY DECORATION

Strings of spices and dried oranges threaded on to raffia make attractive decorations all the year round.

MATERIALS

secateurs
cinnamon sticks
dried oranges
picture framer's gilt wax
raffia
large-eyed needle
large dried chillies
dried bay leaves
scissors

2 Unthread the needle and wrap one end of raffia twice around three cinnamon sticks and the other end twice around in the other direction. Bring the ends of raffia together and tie tightly.

1 Cut the cinnamon sticks to about 10cm/4in long and gild the oranges with gilt wax. Then wind a piece of raffia around a bundle of three cinnamon sticks and tie it in a bow for the bottom of the decoration. Next feed a separate piece of raffia through the original piece, make sure the ends are even and then thread them on to the needle. Thread on three chillies, one orange and 20 bay leaves.

3 Re-thread the needle and thread on three chillies, an orange and 20 bay leaves. Unthread the needle and tie on the cinnamon sticks, as in step 2. Continue until the desired length is reached.

CLOVE-STUDDED CANDLE AND HOLDER

This clove-studded beeswax candle has an Elizabethan look, reminiscent of the the tall and elegant chimneys of the era. Team it with a simple, co-ordinated holder, for a pretty tablecentre or sideboard decoration.

MATERIALS
dry florist's foam ball, about 15cm/6in diameter
large kitchen knife
about 25 star anise
florist's reel wire
scissors
beeswax candle, 5cm/2in diameter
bradawl, knitting needle or skewer
cloves

1 Cut the bottom third off the foam ball with a large knife. Wire each of the star anise by passing two pieces of florist's wire, each about 7.5cm/3in long, over the top and twisting them together at the back. This creates an attractive cross on the front of the star anise, bringing a glint of light to the overall design.

2 Make a hole for each clove, using a bradawl, skewer or similar point, in the honeycomb sections of the beeswax, every other honeycomb "cell" down and every third spiralling line of "cells" apart. Insert the cloves in the holes.

3 Push the candle into the middle of the foam-ball section and stud with cloves. Add star anise around the top and bottom circumferences.

SHAKER-STYLE SPICE WREATH

Inspired by herbal gifts made by Shaker communities, this flexible wreath has none of the stiffness of willow-based wreaths. The idea can also be adapted for garlands, to decorate a celebration table, perhaps: just continue threading until you have the length you need and don't join the ends.

MATERIALS

picture framer's gilt wax
dried oranges
natural raffia
cinnamon sticks
large-eyed needle
dried bay leaves

1 Start by rubbing picture framer's gilt wax on to the oranges. Wind a strand of raffia several times around a bundle of three cinnamon sticks, leaving a long tail which will be used for the finishing tie. Thread a single piece of raffia under the original tie, at the opposite side to the knot. Make sure that its ends are even and then knot them securely, as close to the cinnamon bundle as possible.

LEFT: The two ends of raffia are simply tied to complete the wreath.

2 Thread both ends of raffia into the needle and then thread on about 20 bay leaves, then an orange, then 20 more leaves. Unthread the needle and wind the raffia strands twice around three cinnamon sticks in both directions. Tie to secure.

3 Re-thread the needle and continue as above until the garland is 85cm/34in long. Finally, tie the two ends of raffia together in a reef knot. Trim the ends.

AROMATIC HOT MAT

Fill a robust ticking sachet with cloves, to create a charming, aromatic hot mat. Hot pans put on to it straight from the stove will release the unmistakable and tantalizing scent of cloves.

MATERIALS
50cm/¹/₂yd ticking
tape measure
dressmaker's scissors
needle and matching thread
dressmaker's pins
cloves
heavy-duty upholstery needle
cotton string

2 Cut two rectangles of ticking 28 × 23cm/11 × 9in. Place right-sides together. Fold the hanger in half and sandwich between the two main pieces just below the seam allowance, with the raw ends aligning with the raw ends of a short edge.

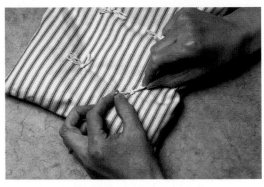

4 Thread the upholstery needle with cotton string and make a stitch about a third of the way in from two adjacent sides of the cushion. Make a simple knot. Untwist the strands of string. Repeat for the other three ties.

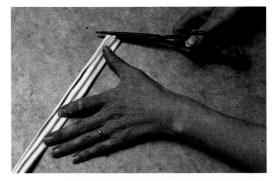

1 Make the hanging loop by folding a strip of ticking 5 × 30cm/2 × 12in in half lengthways, wrong sides together. Trim and turn in the raw edges and stitch the long seam.

3 Pin and stitch together, leaving a 10cm/4in gap. Turn right-sides out and fill loosely with cloves – if you overfill it will make an unsteady mat. Slip-stitch to close.

CINNAMON AND PEPPERTREE BERRY POT

The vibrant combination of red peppertree berries and cinnamon sticks makes for an extrovert container.

MATERIALS
secateurs
cinnamon sticks
small terracotta flower pot
glue gun and hot wax glue
red peppertree berries
small glass jar (optional)

1 Using secateurs, cut each of the cinnamon sticks to exactly fit the height of the flower pot.

2 Using the glue gun, run a line of glue down one cinnamon stick and fix it to the pot. Repeat with the other cinnamon sticks, until they are placed evenly all around the pot, judging the distances with your eye as you go.

3 Using the hot wax glue and glue gun fill the space between two cinnamon sticks with glue.

4 Sprinkle on the peppertree berries. Put a small jar (such as a baby-food jar) into the pot, if you want to use it for cut flowers. Alternatively you could use the pot as a decorative container for pencils and paint brushes.

CHAPTER FIVE

AROMATIC SPICES

THERE IS NO LACK OF HENNA AND NARD, OF SAFFRON,

CALAMUS AND CINNAMON OR INCENSE OF EVERY

KIND. MYRRH AND ALOES GROW THERE WITH ALL THE

MOST FRAGRANT PERFUMES.

SONG OF SOLOMON 4:14

ABOVE: Traditional pomanders are a decorative way to naturally scent the room.

LEFT: The rich, pungent aromas of spices, free from lighter and sometimes cloying floral notes, make popular bath and aromatherapy treats for men and women alike.

Rich and spicy fragrances can be every-day luxuries for us all, promoting a sense of well-being and instantly evoking a time, a place, a mood. What a treat, then, to have a home lightly perfumed with the natural scents of spices, pervading our rooms, freshening our drawers and cupboards and filling our bathrooms. The woman in the

BELOW: Spicy fragrances for body and bath are universally popular.

book of Proverbs in the Bible knew exactly what she was doing when she said "I have perfumed my bed with myrrh, aloes and cinnamon", using the aromas of spices to create an inviting environment just as we do with an essential oil burner. The aromatic smell of spices has a universal attraction, transcending time, gender and nationality. Yet often our spices stay firmly in kitchen cupboards to fulfil their prime task of flavouring, while leaving the job of scenting to flowers and herbs, which generally have a lighter, less enduring note.

In centuries past, the main reason for using herbs and spices to perfume the air was very much down-to-earth. Lack of sanitation and personal hygiene meant that ambient odours were pretty unpleasant and these needed to be counteracted by bowls of pot

Warning
Even natural products can cause allergies in some people. Test skin products on a small patch of skin before putting them into general use. Pregnant women should avoid all home-made cosmetics, unless under the guidance of an expert.

ABOVE: Before you light candles drop some essential spice oil in the top to scent the room.

pourri in the home. Many people also carried pomanders, to sweeten the air wherever they went. Modern hygiene has, thankfully, released us from the need to perfume ourselves and our homes for such prosaic reasons, but it is still true that pleasant aromas can greatly increase the sense of well-being.

The aromatic potential of spices in the home is huge, ranging from the mellow, rounded perfume of nutmeg and mace to

ABOVE: A selection of spice oils. Inhalation of cinnamon improves the appetite and relieves the symptoms of influenza; cardamom has a fresh fragrance that can be used to perfume cosmetics; and cloves are good for relieving indigestion and toothache. Put a few drops of your choice into a steaming bowl of water, lean over and inhale.

warm and exotic cinnamon and cassia, fresh and subtle cardamom and rich, pungent cloves. Their enduring qualities provide the perfect ingredients for scenting rooms, drawers and cupboards and making bathroom treats such as soaps and moisturizers.

Over the next few pages, there are plenty of ideas, ranging from the centuries-old traditions with a fresh, contemporary twist to new ideas for linen and room scenters, to easy-to-make spicy cosmetics. While everything made with spices exudes its own distinctive aroma, these projects lend a little luxury to everyday life.

FRAGRANT DRAWER-SCENTER

A deliciously sumptuous cardamom-filled drawer sachet, made from a rich combination of shot organza, velvet and chenille, makes a witty alternative to the traditional lavender bag.

MATERIALS
pencil and tracing paper
dressmaker's scissors
scrap of velvet
0.5m/¹/2 yd gold-shot organza
tape measure
needle, tacking (basting) and matching thread
sewing machine
handful cardamom pods
28 x 15cm/6in lengths of chenille
large-eyed needle

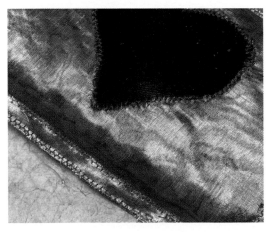

❧ 1 ❧ Trace the small heart template from the back of the book. Use this to cut one velvet heart. Cut four pieces of organza 21 × 15cm/8 × 6in. Tack (baste) the heart to the centre of one organza rectangle. Put this on top of another rectangle and machine straight-stitch around the edge with the matching thread. Set the machine on close zig zag and use this to appliqué the heart in position. Remove the tacking (basting). Straight-stitch the other two organza rectangles together. You have now completed the back and front of the sachet.

LEFT: The soft velvet heart makes a sensuous contrast to the shiny organza.

❧ 2 ❧ Place the back and front sections of the sachet right sides together. Stitch round three sides, leaving a side open. Turn right-sides out and fill with cardamom pods. Slip-stitch to close. Using close zig zag, stitch all around the outside and again, 5mm/¹/4 in inside that line.

❧ 3 ❧ Take the lengths of chenille, fold one of them in half, thread both ends through the needle and pass through a corner.

4 Unthread the needle, make sure the loop is level with the two loose ends, gather all four together and make a simple knot, as close as you can to the edge of the sachet. Repeat with all the other pieces of chenille, until you have fringes of 14 pieces of chenille per side. Trim the ends so that they are all the same length.

SPICY WARDROBE-SCENTER

This fabulous, sequin-studded wardrobe-scenter is fitted with a loop to hang on a dress hanger. The pungent aroma of cloves will perfume the whole cupboard.

MATERIALS
tracing paper and pencil
scissors
dressmaker's pins
0.5m/1/2 yd slubbed silk
dressmaker's scissors
needle
gold thread
40 gold sequins, 8mm/5/8 in diameter
40 glass beads, 3mm/1/8 in diameter
1.5m/1 1/2 yd taffeta ribbon, 2.5cm/1in wide
matching thread
2 handfuls cloves

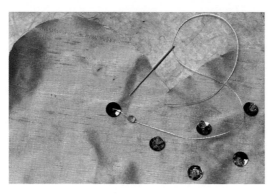

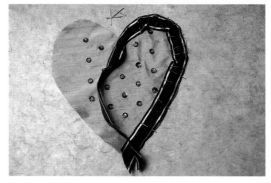

1 Trace the large heart from the back of the book and cut it out. Pin this pattern on the slubbed silk and cut out two hearts. Thread the needle with gold thread and knot the end. Pass the needle from the back of the fabric about 3cm/1¼ in below the dip in the heart. Thread on one sequin and one bead.

2 Bring the gold thread over the side of the bead and down through the sequin again to the back of the fabric. Bring the needle up again about 3cm/1¼ in below the first bead and repeat. Make a vertical row of four beads altogether down the centre of the heart. In the same way, make two more rows to the right of the centre and two to the left, always starting 3cm/1¼ in below the top edge. Repeat with the other heart.

3 Pin the ribbon to the right side of one heart shape, as shown, taking in tucks, where necessary, around the curves. Allow both ends to project beyond the bottom point. Reserve some ribbon for a hanger.

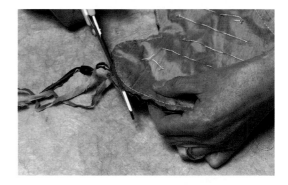

4 Lay the other heart, face-down, on top of the first and pin it in position. Leaving the bottom point free, stitch around the heart. Trim the seams and clip into the seam allowance at the curves.

5 Turn right sides out and fill with cloves. Turn the ends of the ribbon in at the bottom point, folding one end over the other to make a neat finish. Fold in the raw edges of the bottom of the heart and then hand-sew to close. Fold the remaining ribbon in half. Turn in the ends and then sew the loop to the back of the heart, where it dips in the middle.

AROMATIC PADDED HANGERS

Sweetly scented cassia bark makes a fabulous perfumed filling for padded coathangers. They are very easy to make by hand: the perfect gift idea for fund-raising stalls.

MATERIALS FOR EACH HANGER

0.5m/1/2 yd grosgrain ribbon
wooden coathanger
needle and matching thread
dressmaker's scissors
heavyweight wadding (batting), a little longer
than the hanger and 15cm/6in wide
cassia bark
brocade, 1½ times the length of the hanger and
20cm/8in wide
dressmaker's pins

BELOW: Cinnamon-coloured brocade and mustard ribbon add up to a rich, spicy combination.

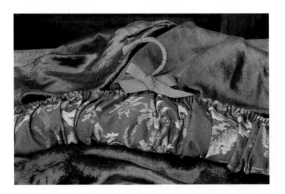

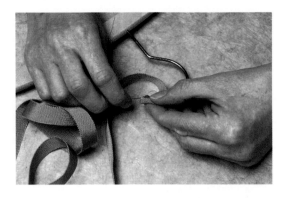

1 Wind the end of the ribbon around the end of the hanger hook and stitch it, to secure. Continue to bind the ribbon around the hook and stitch the bottom end to secure.

3 Wrap the wadding (batting) around the hanger and stitch to secure, pulling the wadding tightly around the hanger as you go to make a neat shape. Fold in the ends and stitch neatly.

2 Lay the hanger on the wadding (batting) and lay the cassia bark under the curve, making sure there are no sharp bits sticking out. It is best to lay all the pieces lengthways along the hanger.

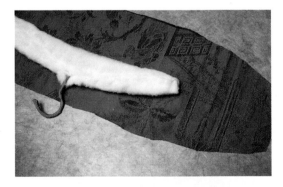

4 Trim the corners off the brocade to create a gentle curve. Fold the brocade in half across the width and mark the middle of each long edge with a pin. This marks the position of the hanging hook.

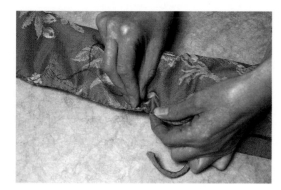

5 Wrap the brocade around the hanger. Turn in the raw edges at one end and using double thread, stitch along the edges, turning them in as you go from one end to the middle, matching the pins at the centre.

6 Pull the threads to gather the brocade to fit round the hanger and fasten off securely. Repeat with the other end of the hanger. Decorate with a bow on the handle, made from the remaining ribbon.

SPICE POT POURRI

Spice pot pourri makes a refreshing alternative to the more normal flower-based pot pourri. Choose the bigger spices, to lend colour and texture, and spice powders to add to the richness of the perfume.

MATERIALS
handful mace
handful cloves
handful cardamom pods
handful cinnamon sticks, about 5cm/2in long
6 star anise
5 dried orange slices
15g/¹/2 oz orris root powder
5ml/1 tsp ground cloves
5ml/1 tsp ground nutmeg
pestle and mortar
5ml/1 tsp cinnamon oil
5ml/1 tsp orange oil
4ml/3/4 tsp clove oil
screw-topped glass jars
large mixing bowl

1 Put the mace, cloves, cardamom, cinnamon sticks, star anise and orange slices in your display container, to check that the quantities will fit.

3 Add a few drops of the oil mixture to the spice powders. Seal in a glass jar. Mix the rest of the oils with the cloves and cardamom. Seal in another jar.

2 Mix the orris root and ground spices together in a pestle and mortar. Blend all the oils together in one jar.

4 The next day, put the rest of the materials in a large bowl. Add the oily cloves and cardamom pods and mix well. Repeat with the crumbly powders. Seal in a glass jar and leave to mature in a dark place for up to six weeks before use.

CLASSIC POMANDERS

Pomanders have been a favourite Christmas decoration since Elizabethan times; there is still something irresistible about the classic pomanders, made with dried oranges stuck with cloves. However, the traditional method of making them with fixatives and slow drying times taking up to four weeks can be tricky; a race against time before they turn mouldy. Here is an easier, rather more reliable method, done in 12 hours in the oven.

MATERIALS
navel or thin-skinned oranges
ball-point pen (optional)
cloves
bradawl or knitting needle (optional)
scalpel or sharp craft knife
skewers

1 Preheat the oven to 50°C/100°F/ Gas ½. Work out your own design of lines, spirals, or lace effects and, if you prefer, draw this on the skin of the orange first with a ball-point pen. Then insert the cloves. If you can't get navel or other thin-skinned oranges, you'll need to make holes first, using a bradawl or knitting needle. Don't make the holes too deep or the cloves will fall out.

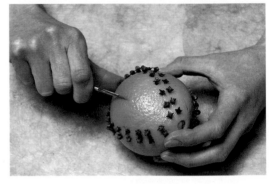

2 Cut slits between the cloves. At this point, the slits will not show.

3 Put the oranges on skewers and hang directly in the oven, so there is plenty of air circulating around them. Leave for 12 hours, or until the oranges are fully dried.

LEFT: Some of the simplest designs are also the most effective.

CARDAMOM POMANDERS

Decorative pomanders can be made from almost any spice, glued on to dry florist's foam balls. Here, the muted shades of green cardamom pods enliven the earthy browns of cloves. The green will fade over time and the pomanders will turn to an equally pleasing coffee and cream.

MATERIALS FOR EACH
POMANDER
handful cloves
dry florist's foam ball, about 7.5cm/3in diameter
glue gun and hot wax glue
handful cardamom pods

BELOW: For each pomander, you need a handful each of cloves and cardamoms.

1 Begin by pressing the cloves directly into the foam ball, making a circle right around it. Make another circle at right angles to the first.

2 Make another row of cloves on each side of both circles, so the ball is quartered by a three-cloves-thick band. Place the cloves close together to cover all the foam.

3 Using the glue gun, carefully apply adhesive along one side of each cardamom pod, and attach it to the ball. Repeat, filling one quarter from the top down. Repeat with the other three quarters. Work methodically, carefully placing each cardamom pod longitudinally in the quarter, ensuring you completely cover the foam.

Make pomanders up in several different designs, for interest. These instructions show you how to make a pomander that is quartered vertically by cloves and filled in with cardamom pods. The pomander in the foreground has concentric circles of cloves and cardamoms. Plan your design before you begin.

SCENTED TOILETRIES BAG

The sweet scent and gentle tones of green cardamom pods make this ribbon-trimmed silk toiletries bag very special indeed. Despite its sophisticated look, it is not difficult to make: the key is in choosing pretty, toning ribbons. The bag is simply tied at the top with rayon ribbon. You can quickly and easily adapt this into a drawstring by stitching on a small brass ring about 2.5cm/1in below the top of each vertical seam and thread the ribbon through this.

MATERIALS

tracing paper and pencil
dressmaker's scissors
1m/1yd cream dress silk
dressmaker's pins
2.25m/2½ yd scalloped-edge ribbon,
3.5cm/1½ in wide
4.5m/5yd organza ribbon, 5cm/2in wide
sewing machine
matching thread
4 handfuls cardamom pods
2m/2yd contrasting rayon ribbon, 1cm/½ in wide
small brass rings (optional)

1 Trace the template from the back of the book and use it as a pattern. Cut four main pieces and four facing pieces in silk. Pin the scalloped-edge ribbon to the centre of each main and facing piece.

2 On either side of this, pin a length of organza ribbon, so the inside edge lies under the scallops. Stitch down both sides of organza ribbon and then top-stitch the scalloped-edge ribbon.

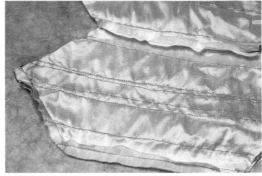

3 With right sides together, stitch the long side seams of the main pieces until all the seams of the bag are joined. With right sides together, begin to join the base by stitching adjacent seams (see left of picture). Turn right sides out.

4 Fill the channels made by the organza ribbon with cardamom pods, until they reach about a third up the channel.

5 With right sides together, stitch the side seams of the facings and then make a hem at the bottom and stitch.

6 With right sides together, match the diagonal edges of the facings to the diagonal edges of the top of the bag. Stitch along all diagonals. Trim the seams, cut off the points of the triangles within the seam allowance and then turn right sides out. Tie the bag at the neck with a rayon ribbon, to close, allowing the points to turn back decoratively.

CITRUS MOISTURIZER

Make your own deliciously fresh lime moisturizer and then package it up in pretty glass bottles, to give as gifts. While not strictly a spice, lime has an equally pungent quality. It is a mild astringent.

MATERIALS FOR 4 SMALL JARS

2 heatproof mixing bowls

small saucepan

20ml/4 tsp beeswax granules

25g/1 oz cocoa butter

80ml/5 tbsp almond oil

wooden spoon

10ml/2 tsp borax

180ml/6fl oz/¾ cup orange flower water

10 drops lime essential oil

Caution

As with all cosmetic preparations, this moisturizer may cause an allergic reaction in some people. Do not give this preparation to a pregnant woman. As with all citrus preparations, do not use before using a sunbed or going into strong sun.

1 Put a bowl over a saucepan of simmering water and add the beeswax, cocoa butter and almond oil. Warm, stirring gently, until all the ingredients have completely dissolved.

2 In another bowl mix together the borax and orange flower water. Place over the saucepan of simmering water and gently dissolve.

3 Take off the heat and slowly pour the borax and orange flower water into the bowl of wax, stirring all the time.

4 Add the lime essential oil. Pour into small jars and keep refrigerated. Dispose of any cream left over after three weeks.

GINGER BODYSCRUB

Ginger, with its invigorating aroma, stimulates the circulation and so makes an excellent additive for a bodyscrub. The clays and honey will draw any impurities out of the skin, and the orange flower water will add fragrance. Keep in the fridge and use within three weeks.

MATERIALS
2 small bowls
20ml/4 tsp kaolin
10ml/2 tsp green clay
15ml/1 tbsp ground almonds
15ml/1 tbsp clear honey
30ml/2 tbsp warm water
15ml/1 tbsp orange flower water
3 drops ginger essential oil
small spoon
glass storage jar

1 In one of the bowls, place the kaolin, green clay and ground almonds. In the other bowl, dissolve the honey in the water and then add the orange flower water and essential oil.

2 Slowly pour the honey, water, orange flower and oil mixture into the kaolin, clay and ground almonds mixture.

3 Blend, using the spoon. Store in a glass jar in the fridge for up to four weeks. To use, massage on to the skin in circular movements, adding a little water if necessary. Rinse off with warm water. It is best either to use up all the scrub in one treatment, or store it in glass jars, as glass is inert and will not affect the chemical make-up of the scrub.

> ### *Caution*
> As with all skin preparations, this may cause an allergic reaction in some people. Do not use if pregnant.

LEMONGRASS SOAP

Lemongrass has toning and antiseptic qualities that not only help relieve oily skin and acne, but can also help tighten up loose post-pregnancy or post-diet skin.

MATERIALS TO MAKE 2 BARS

grater

150g/5oz bar of unscented soap

heatproof bowl

measuring jug

saucepan

spoon

pestle and mortar

12 drops lemongrass essential oil

BELOW: Papyrus and raffia make wonderful natural wrapping for lemongrass soap. Tuck in some fresh or dried lemongrass to make a gift.

1 Using the finest side of a cheese grater, grate the soap into a bowl.

2 Add water in the proportion of one part water to two parts soap. Put the bowl over a saucepan of simmering water and stir the mixture continuously, until it coalesces. You will see this happening slowly and the soap will become thicker, gradually getting harder to mix. Remove the pan from the heat.

3 Tip the soap into a pestle and mortar and add the lemongrass oil. Mix well.

4 Wet your hands, take about half the soap and work into a bar. Repeat to make another bar. Leave on a wooden board to dry out and set hard. This may take a couple of days. Use within a month.

CHAPTER SIX

DELICIOUS
SPICY GIFTS

Nose, nose, jolly red nose,

And who gave thee this jolly red nose?…

Nutmegs and ginger, cinnamon and cloves,

And they gave me this jolly red nose.

JOHN FLETCHER (1579–1625), THE KNIGHT OF THE BURNING PESTLE

Above: Packed into a pretty wooden box, ginger truffles make a special gift.

Left: Scrumptious spiced treats – such as Spiced Pickled Pears – will be welcomed by everyone.

101

We would soon tire of the bland taste of dishes lacking the piquancy of spices and, nowadays, we have a huge range of spices, both dried and fresh, at our disposal. Though the journey from their place of origin to our local supermarket has been somewhat less dramatic than in the days of the spice trails across oceans and continents, the treat, in terms of the flavour they hold, is not diminished. Many of the gifts in the

following pages echo a tradition with roots in the eighteenth century, when pickles and relishes were brought back from India. These flavour-packed jars of sauces, such as chutney and piccalilli, were used to add extra flavour to cooked dishes.

It is easy to turn these spicy storecupboard

LEFT: Cinnamon sticks and mace both have subtle, rounded flavours.

ABOVE: Peppercorns, bay and cardamom are three popular pickling spices.

treats into very special gifts by searching out attractive packaging: preserving jars in attractive shapes; country baskets; and pretty painted boxes which can be lined with co-ordinated fabrics. Then, when the contents have long been finished, the container can be used again and again.

ABOVE: Cinnamon tea is a refreshing and therapeutic drink, helping to relieve colds.

Who would not be delighted with a delicious treat flavoured with aromatic spices and packaged specially for giving and storing? Even those who seem to have everything will enjoy delicately spicy sweets and biscuits (cookies); mustards and chutneys packed with flavour, and piquant biscuits and fruit. Gifts such as these are even more valued when they have been specially prepared and beautifully presented for that person.

Most of the recipes in this chapter can be made up in batches, attractively gift-wrapped and given as Christmas or birthday gifts. They are bound to be popular, since exquisitely flavoured foods have a universal appeal.

SPICY DRINKS

Warming, spicy drinks are a welcome treat on cold days and many have therapeutic qualities. Here are three favourites, which could be packed into gift baskets to take to friends when visiting as house guests. You could write the recipe by hand on to a co-ordinating label, so the recipients would immediately know how to put the drink together.

GINGERED HOT TODDY

Gingered hot toddy is not only delicious and warming, it can relieve the early symptoms of influenza if taken at night, just before you go to sleep.

INGREDIENTS

In each kit, include: jar of stem ginger; jar of honey; a lemon; and a small bottle of whisky.

TO MAKE

Finely slice one piece of stem ginger and then put it in a heatproof glass with 10ml/ 2 tsp clear honey and a slice of lemon. Two-thirds fill with boiling water, add the whisky and stir in lemon juice to taste. Sip while piping hot for a warming, therapeutic effect just before you drift off.

ABOVE: Make a gift presentation of gingered hot toddy, by topping the ginger and honey with gold organza and pouring the whisky into a miniature decanter; then pile everything into a pretty wire basket.

RIGHT: Red gold organza with a golden tie makes a sumptuous festive wrapping that teams with the golden hues of honey.

CINNAMON TEA

A most refreshing and aromatic beverage, this is delicious at the best of times but also helps speed convalescence from 'flu, relieving nausea, chills, congestion and general aches and pains.

INGREDIENTS

In each kit, include: lemon-scented tea bags; cinnamon sticks; oranges; demerara (brown) sugar.

TO MAKE

Into a heatproof glass, put a tea bag, cinnamon stick and slice of orange. Top up with boiling water and stir with the cinnamon stick, until the tea has reached the desired strength. Discard the tea bag and add one or two teaspoons of demerara (brown) sugar, to taste.

MULLED WINE

Little evokes the Christmas spirit more than a traditional glass of aromatic, spicy mulled wine, served piping hot.

INGREDIENTS FOR 6 PEOPLE

In each kit, include: a bottle of wine; orange juice, decanted into an attractive screw-topped jar or bottle; a jar of demerara (brown) sugar; cinnamon sticks; clementines, studded with cloves.

LEFT: Lend an Asian feel to cinnamon tea by packing it into a Chinese cane basket. Wrap the tea bags in glassine paper and decant the demerara sugar into a pretty glass bottle.

ABOVE: The robust, country flavour of mulled wine can be complemented by a country-style presentation. Line an old basket with brocade and then pack clove-studded clementines into a decorative jar and add to the basket.

TO MAKE

Pour the bottle of wine into a saucepan and add 250ml/8fl oz/1 cup of orange juice, 60ml/4 tbsp of demerara (brown) sugar and two cinnamon sticks, halved. Quarter the clove-studded clementines and add to the pan. Slowly bring the wine to the boil, leave to stand for 15 minutes and then reheat and ladle into heatproof glasses.

SPICED PICKLED PEARS

These pears, spiced with cardamom, are delicious with cold roast meats and salad.

INGREDIENTS
30ml/2 tbsp lemon juice
2kg/4½ lb pears
2 × 350ml/12fl oz bottles red wine vinegar
1kg/2¼ lb/5 cups granulated sugar
10ml/2 tsp cardamom pods
10ml/2 tsp whole black peppercorns
3 bay leaves
3 strips orange rind

MAKES 3 MEDIUM JARS

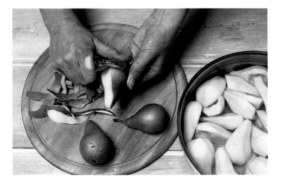

1 Half-fill a large saucepan or preserving pan with cold water and add the lemon juice. Discard the pear stalks and then peel and halve the pears and cut out the cores. Immediately place into the pan.

Storage
Do not consume for at least two weeks. Keep in a cool, dark place for up to three months. Once opened, pickled pears should be stored in the fridge.

2 Bring the water to the boil and then cook the pears for 15 minutes, or until tender. Drain in a colander. Pour the vinegar into the pan and add the sugar. Split the cardamom pods, roughly crush the peppercorns and add the spices to the vinegar, with the bay leaves and orange rind. Bring to the boil and simmer until the sugar has dissolved. Return the pears to the pan and leave to simmer for 10 minutes, turning the fruit several times, so that it cooks evenly.

3 Lift the pears out with a slotted spoon and pack into warm, dry, sterilized jars. Strain the vinegar into the jars, making sure the pears are well covered. Add the bay leaves and orange rind and wedge the fruit below the surface of the vinegar with crumpled pieces of greaseproof paper. Seal well and leave to cool.

Sterilizing Jars
To sterilize jars for preserves, wash them thoroughly in very hot, soapy water and rinse and dry them well. Put them upside down in a warm oven to dry for about 30 minutes.

MELLOW GOLDEN APPLE AND TOMATO CHUTNEY

This mellow, golden, spicy chutney transforms a ploughman's lunch.

INGREDIENTS
1.5kg/3lb cooking apples
1.5kg/3lb tomatoes
2 large onions
2 garlic cloves
250g/9oz stoned (pitted) dates
2 red peppers
3 dried red chillies
15ml/1 tbsp black peppercorns
4 cardamom pods
15ml/1 tbsp coriander seeds
10ml/2 tsp cumin seeds
10ml/2 tsp turmeric
15ml/1 tbsp salt
600ml/1 pint/2½ cups distilled malt vinegar
1kg/2¼ lb/5 cups granulated sugar

MAKES ABOUT 4 JARS

Storage
Store for up to two weeks before tasting. Store unopened jars for up to a year, in a cool, dark place. Once opened, store the chutney in the fridge.

1 Quarter, core, peel and chop the apples. Peel and chop the tomatoes, onions and garlic. Quarter the dates. Core and de-seed the peppers, then cut into chunky pieces. Put all the prepared ingredients, except the red peppers, into a preserving pan.

2 Slit the chillies. Put the peppercorns and remaining spices into a pestle and mortar and roughly crush. Add all prepared spices, the turmeric and salt to the pan.

3 Pour in the vinegar and sugar and bring to the boil, stirring. Leave to simmer for 30 minutes, stirring occasionally. Add the red pepper and cook for a further 30 minutes, stirring more frequently as the chutney becomes thick and pulpy.

4 Spoon into warm, dry, sterilized jars, using a jam funnel to catch any spills. Cover with a waxed disc and vinegar-proof lid. Leave to cool.

AROMATIC SPICED PEACHES

A great gift for friends who hate cooking, this indulgent dessert is luscious served with scoops of luxury vanilla ice cream or Greek yogurt, flavoured with honey and chopped glacé ginger.

INGREDIENTS
500g/1lb 2oz/2½ cups granulated sugar
2 cinnamon sticks
4 star anise
1kg/2¼ lb/12 peaches
300ml/½ pint/1¼ cups brandy

MAKES 1.5 LITRES/3 PINTS

BELOW: Two delicious, spicy, bottled fruits in the same basic syrup. Make up batches and then give one of each to busy friends.

1 Put 300ml/½ pint/1¼ cups of water into a saucepan, add the sugar and heat until dissolved. Boil for 2 minutes. Break the cinnamon sticks in two and add them to the syrup, with the star anise. Halve and stone the peaches and add them to the syrup. Bring the syrup back to the boil, cover and leave to simmer for 5 minutes, turning the peaches once or twice, to ensure even cooking.

2 Lift the peaches out with a draining spoon and pack into two warm, dry, sterilized jars, with the spices. Boil the remaining sugar syrup rapidly for 5 minutes. Pour into the jars to half-fill them and then top up with brandy, making sure that it covers the fruit well. Add a piece of crumpled greaseproof paper to keep the fruit beneath the syrup and then seal well and leave to cool.

Variation
CINNAMON-SPICED CHERRIES
Make the syrup as above and spice with only 3 cinnamon sticks. Remove the stalks and stones from 1kg/2¼ lb of cherries, poach in the syrup for 2 minutes and then continue as for the peaches, above.

Storage
Keep in a cool, dark place for up to six months before opening. You may find the fruit will rise to begin with but, as it becomes saturated with the syrup, it will sink back again to the bottom of the jar. Once opened, keep the peaches in the fridge.

SPICY MUSTARDS

Delicious, aromatic home-made mustards mature to the most fragrant of relishes for sausages, grilled steaks or boiled ham.

CLOVE-SPICED MUSTARD

INGREDIENTS
75g/3oz white mustard seeds
50g/2oz/1/4 cup soft light brown sugar
5ml/1 tsp salt
5ml/1 tsp black peppercorns
5ml/1 tsp cloves
5ml/1 tsp turmeric
200ml/7fl oz/7/8 cup distilled malt vinegar

MAKES 300ML/1/2 PINT/11/4 CUPS

2 Gradually add the vinegar, 15ml/1tbsp at a time, blending well between each tablespoon, then continue blending until you have a coarse paste.

1 Put the mustard seeds, sugar, salt, peppercorns, cloves and turmeric into a liquidizer and blend together.

LEFT: Glassine paper makes a smart top for small glass jars. Tie with string for a rustic look, and tuck an ingredient in for decoration if you are giving it away

3 Leave to stand for 10–15 minutes, to thicken slightly. Spoon into a 300ml/ 1/2 pint jar or several smaller jars, using a funnel. Cover the surface of the mustard with a waxed paper disc and then seal with a screw-topped lid, or cork, and label.

GARLIC AND CHILLI MUSTARD

INGREDIENTS

40g/1¹/2 oz white mustard seeds
40g/1¹/2 oz black mustard seeds
50g/2oz/¹/4 cup soft light brown sugar
5ml/1 tsp salt
5ml/1 tsp whole peppercorns
10ml/2 tsp tomato purée
1 dried red chilli
1 large garlic clove
200ml/7fl oz/⁷/8 cup distilled malt vinegar

MAKES 300ML/¹/2 PINT/1¹/4 CUPS

Make up as for Clove-spiced Mustard.

BELOW, FROM LEFT: Pink peppercorn mustard, moutarde aux fines herbes, and garlic and chilli mustard, a fine array for any pantry.

PINK PEPPERCORN MUSTARD

INGREDIENTS

75g/3oz white mustard seeds
50g/2oz/¹/4 cup soft light brown sugar
5ml/1 tsp salt
1.25ml/¹/4 tsp turmeric
200ml/7fl oz/⁷/8 cup distilled malt vinegar
15ml/1 tbsp whole pink peppercorns

MAKES 300ML/¹/2 PINT/1¹/4 CUPS

Put the mustard seeds, sugar, salt and turmeric into a liquidizer. Blend them and then gradually add the vinegar, until you have a thick paste. Add the pink peppercorns and blend briefly, until coarsely mixed.
Continue as for Clove-spiced Mustard.

ABOVE: Package the mustards in jars topped by pretty fabric scraps, for a hand-made signature.

MOUTARDE AUX FINES HERBES

INGREDIENTS

75g/3oz white mustard seeds
50g/2oz/¹/4 cup soft light brown sugar
5ml/1 tsp salt
5ml/1 tsp whole peppercorns
2.5ml/¹/2 tsp turmeric
200ml/7fl oz/⁷/8 cup distilled malt vinegar
60ml/4 tbsp chopped fresh mixed herbs,
e.g. parsley, sage, thyme and rosemary

MAKES 300ML/¹/2 PINT/1¹/4 CUPS

Make up as for Clove-spiced Mustard, adding the herbs at the very end.

SPICED FETA CHEESE WITH OLIVES

M arinated cubes of feta, spiked with spices and olives, make the ideal gift for salad-lovers. They make a delicious summer dressing with the added bulk of the extra cheese. Simply spoon over green leaves and serve with warm crusty bread for a quick and nutritious Mediterranean-inspired summer lunch or a light starter.

INGREDIENTS
500g/1lb 2oz feta cheese
50g/2oz stuffed olives
10ml/2 tsp coriander seeds
10ml/2 tsp whole peppercorns
5ml/1 tsp chilli seeds
few sprigs fresh rosemary or thyme
750ml/1¼ pint/3 cups virgin olive oil

MAKES 5 ASSORTED SMALL JARS

Storage
The spiced feta cheese with olives can be kept in airtight jars in the fridge for up to three weeks.

1 Drain and dice the feta cheese and put it in a bowl. Slice the olives. Crush the coriander seeds and peppercorns in a pestle and mortar and then add them to the cheese, with the olives, chilli seeds and rosemary or thyme leaves. Toss lightly.

2 Spoon the cheese into warm, dry, sterilized jars and top up with olive oil, making sure that the cheese is well covered by the oil. Seal with screw-topped or clip-down lids. The jars need to be completely airtight to keep the cheese fresh.

LEFT: Small, square preserving jars make attractive packaging for this pretty summer dressing, echoing the shape of the feta cubes.

SPICED OILS AND VINEGARS

Oils and vinegars flavoured with whole and freshly ground spices bring piquancy to any recipe. They make the perfect gift for keen cooks and an attractive and exotic addition to any kitchen shelf.

Use to pep up plain salad dressings, drizzle the oil over bruschetta-style toppings on toast or use to fry steaks or chicken. Flavour slow-cooked casseroles with the vinegar or use it as an instant marinade.

CHILLI-FLAVOURED VINEGAR

INGREDIENTS
6 dried red chillies
10ml/2 tsp black peppercorns
10ml/2 tsp cloves
3 cinnamon sticks
1 litre/1³/4 pints/4 cups red wine vinegar
extra spices, to decorate

MAKES 1 LITRE/1³/4 PINTS/4 CUPS

Storage
Keep oils and vinegars in a cool place for up to three months.

1 Slit the chillies and roughly crush the peppercorns. Put them into a saucepan, with the cloves and halved cinnamon sticks. Dry fry for a minute, to bring out the flavour.

2 Pour on the vinegar and then bring to the boil. Cool and pour into sterilized screw-topped jars. Seal and leave for two weeks in a cool, dark place, turning daily.

3 Strain and decant into pretty, sterilized bottles. Add a fresh cinnamon stick, 2 dried chillies and a few cloves and peppercorns to each. Seal the bottles well with corks or screw-topped lids.

SPICY OLIVE OIL

INGREDIENTS
30ml/2 tbsp coriander seeds
15ml/1 tbsp cumin seeds
15ml/1 tbsp cardamom pods
1 litre/1¾ pints/4 cups extra virgin olive oil
4 bay leaves
extra spices and bay leaves, to decorate

MAKES 1 LITRE/1¾ PINTS/4 CUPS

1 Crush the coriander and cumin seeds roughly, using a pestle and mortar. Split the cardamom pods with the pestle and then put all the spices into a saucepan. Dry fry the spices.

2 Take the pan off the heat and add the oil. Pour into a large, sterilized screw-topped jar or bottle. Add the bay leaves and seal well. Leave for two weeks in a cool, dark place, turning each day.

3 Strain and decant into pretty, sterilized bottles. Add an extra bay leaf and a few whole seeds to each bottle and then seal with corks or screw-topped lids. Finish by tying on some spices and herbs for decoration and identification.

MEDITERRANEAN MARINATED
PEPPERS WITH SPICES

Highly decorative and fragrantly delicious, these peppers can be used as part of a mixed platter of starters, tossed with pasta for a light lunch or quick supper dish; or serve as an accompaniment, as part of a larger meal.

INGREDIENTS

1kg/2¼ lb mixed red, yellow and orange peppers
500ml/18fl oz/2¼ cups extra virgin olive oil
2 garlic cloves
1 cinnamon stick
2.5ml/½ tsp black peppercorns
6 cloves
6 dried red chillies

MAKES 4 SMALL JARS

1 Preheat the grill to hot. Halve, core and de-seed the peppers and cut into chunky pieces. Put them, skin-side up, on a baking sheet. Brush with a little of the oil, then grill until the skins are blackened. Cover with a tea-towel and leave to cool.

2 Put sliced garlic, a halved cinnamon stick and remaining spices into a saucepan, with a little oil. Fry for a minute, add the remaining oil and bring to the boil.

3 While the spices are cooking, peel the skins off the peppers with a small sharp knife and pack the pepper strips into warm, dry sterilized jars. Pour the cooled oil and spices over the peppers, making sure the oil covers them well. Seal with screw-topped lids. If you are giving the peppers as a gift, add a decorative top and label to the jars.

Storage
Keep in an airtight container in the fridge for up to three weeks. Bring to room temperature before serving.

GINGERED TRUFFLES

Wonderfully creamy, these rich choco-late truffles are flecked with ginger, coated in dark chocolate and piped with melted white chocolate, a truly irresistible gift when packed into a pretty box.

INGREDIENTS
150ml/¼ pint/⅔ cup double cream
150g/5oz dark chocolate
25g/1oz/2 tbsp butter
30ml/2 tbsp brandy
15ml/1tbsp glacé ginger or chopped stem ginger

TO FINISH
15ml/1 tbsp cocoa powder
225g/8oz dark chocolate
glacé ginger, chopped
50g/2oz white chocolate

MAKES ABOUT 30 TRUFFLES

1 Put the cream in a heavy-based saucepan and bring it to the boil. Take the pan off the heat. Break the dark chocolate into pieces and add them to the hot cream, with the butter, cut into pieces. Leave to stand for 5 minutes, stirring occasionally, until the chocolate and butter have com-pletely melted. You may need to return the pan to the heat for a few seconds if the chocolate and butter fail to melt completely.

2 Gradually stir in the brandy and then, using an electric whisk, beat for 5–10 min-utes, until the mixture is thick. Finely chop the ginger and stir it in. Cover and chill for 2–3 hours, until firm.

3 Put the cocoa powder on a plate. Lightly dip a teaspoonful of mixture in cocoa and then roll it into a ball with your hands. Put aside. Continue until all the mixture is used up.

> ### *Storage*
> Keep in the fridge for up to two weeks.

4 Freeze the truffles for 30 minutes, or chill for several hours until hard before continuing. Break the remaining dark chocolate into pieces and melt it in a bowl set above a saucepan of very gently simmering water. Do not let the water touch the bowl. Lightly stir the chocolate and then hold a truffle on a fork and spoon chocolate over it, to coat it completely. Carefully transfer to a baking sheet lined with non-stick baking parchment or waxed paper.

5 To finish, roughly chop the ginger, sprinkle it over the truffles and then leave to cool and harden. Melt the white chocolate in the same way. Spoon the chocolate into a greaseproof paper piping bag, snip off the tip and pipe squiggly lines over the truffles. Leave in the fridge to harden. Pack into petit-four cases and arrange in boxes. Cover with a lid or cellophane and tie with ribbon, if you like.

SHAKER-STYLE HONEY-SPICED COOKIES

These delicious spicy cookies can be packed up in pretty boxes, to make elegant gifts for all ages. They are great to give to children or to make with children, as a gift for older relatives.

INGREDIENTS

50g/2oz/4tbsp butter

100g/4oz/scant ½ cup soft light brown sugar

45ml/3 tbsp runny honey

30ml/2 tbsp orange juice or milk

225g/8oz/2 cups plain flour

7.5ml/1½ tsp bicarbonate of soda

5ml/1 tsp ground ginger

1.25ml/¼ tsp ground allspice

1.25ml/¼ tsp ground cinnamon

TO DECORATE

45ml/3 tbsp orange juice or water

100g/4oz/1 cup icing (confectioners') sugar

MAKES ABOUT 25 COOKIES

> ### Storage
> Keep for up to ten days at room temperature.

1 Brush two baking sheets with a little oil and preheat the oven to 160°C/325°F/ Gas 3. Put the butter, sugar and honey into a saucepan and heat gently, stirring occasionally, until the butter has melted.

2 Add the orange juice or milk to the pan. Sift the flour, bicarbonate of soda and spices into the pan and mix with a wooden spoon, until you have a smooth dough. Leave the mixture to cool for 15 minutes. Turn out on to a floured surface, knead lightly and then roll out. Cut out heart and hand shapes, or use cutters.

3 Transfer to baking sheets. Cook for 8–10 minutes, until browned. Leave to cool on the baking sheet, then transfer to a wire rack. To make the icing, gradually mix the orange juice or water with the icing (confectioners') sugar to make a thick paste. Pipe borders of lines and dots, to decorate. Leave to dry overnight, before packing into boxes or tins.

ABOVE: Use heart and hand motifs to make several different shapes.

RIGHT: You could make holes in the dough shapes before cooking and use them as tree decorations.

Tip
Melted white or dark chocolate can be used to decorate the cookies, instead of the icing, if preferred. But eat them within three days, before the chocolate loses its attractive shine.

TEMPLATES

To enlarge the templates, use either a grid system or a photocopier. For the grid system, trace the template and draw a grid of evenly spaced squares over the tracing. Then draw a larger grid on to another piece of paper. Copy the outline on to the second grid, taking each square individually. Draw over the lines to make them continuous.

Fragrant Drawer-scenter
(actual size)

Spicy Wardrobe-scenter
(50% of actual size)

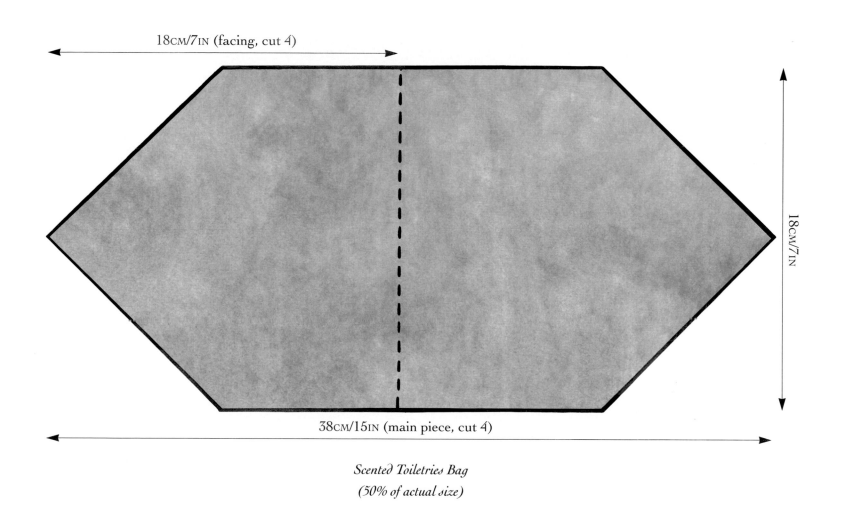

18CM/7IN (facing, cut 4)

18CM/7IN

38CM/15IN (main piece, cut 4)

Scented Toiletries Bag
(50% of actual size)

USEFUL ADDRESSES

UK
Fiddespayne, The Spice Trader,
Pepper Alley, Unit 3b, Thorpe Way, Banbury,
Oxfordshire OX16 8XL
Tel: 01295-253 888
Wholesale spices.

Karin Hossack, 32 Petley Road,
London W6 9ST
Tel: 0171-386 9748
Classic pomanders; also, sculptures in wood and
tin and individually designed handknits.

Cleo Mussi, Unit 72c,
Abbey Business Centre,
15–17 Ingate Place, London SW8 3NS
Tel: 0171-785 2433
Mosaic panels, made to order.

David and Charles Wainwright,
61 Portobello Road, London W11
Tel: 0171-727 0707
251 Portobello Road, London W11
Tel: 0171-792 1988
28 Rosslyn Hill, London NW3
Tel: 0171-431 5900
Shops specializing in antique and modern
furniture and artefacts from India.

The Hop Shop
Castle Farm
Shoreham

Sevenoaks
Kent
Tel: 01959 523919
Suppliers of pot pourri ingredients.

Neal's Yard Remedies
5 Golden Cross
Cornmarket Street
Oxford
OX1 3EU
Tel: 01865 245436 for mail order catalogue.
Suppliers of essential oils.

USA
Tom Thumb Workshops
PO Box 357
Mappsville, VA23407
Tel: (804) 824-3507

The Ultimate Herb & Spice Shoppe
111 Azalea

PO Box 395
Duenweg, MO64841
Tel: (417) 282-0457

Loran Oils
PO Box 22009
Lansing MI48909-2009
Tel: (800) 248 1302

AUSTRALIA
All Asian Food Market
9 Angus Cres
Yagoona
NSW 2199
Tel: (02) 9644 5506
Specializes in spices from India, Pakistan,
Ceylon, Fiji and South Africa.

Fancy Foods
Depot Road
Merriwa
NSW 2329
Tel: (Freecall) 1800 069 516
Supply local and imported herbs and spices.

The Essential Ingredient
4 Australia St
Camperdown
NSW 2050
Tel: (02) 9550 5477
Suppliers of widely used, and more unusual,
spices.

INDEX

ACKNOWLEDGEMENTS

My very special thanks go to everyone who has worked so hard to produce this book: Michelle Garrett, whose evocative photographs so beautifully capture the beguiling quality of spicecrafts, and to her assistant, Dulcie, who looked after us so well on the shoots. Sara Lewis, for her tasty and imaginative recipes for delicious spicy gifts. Karin Hossack, for her most inspired classic pomanders. Helen Sudell for all her support in the most difficult circumstances and her conscientious steering of the project, even when Baby Thomas arrived so many weeks before he was expected. Thanks, too, to Joanne Rippin for taking over the reins and guiding the book through production. Deborah Savage, for her considered and sensitive editing. Nigel Partridge, whose design has turned this book into such a treat. And to everyone whose generosity has contributed to the look of the book.Christopher White, of Fiddespayne, who supplied the spices for the project. David Wainwright, for so generously lending us his house as a location for photographing some of the projects. Cleo Mussi, for lending us her glorious and colourful mosaic as a background for the aromatic spices.